OF MOUSE AND MEN

Confessions of a Disney Character Performer

NICKLAUS HOPKINS

Theme Park Press
The Happiest Books on Earth
www.ThemeParkPress.com

Editor: Bob McLain
Layout: Artisanal Text

ISBN 978-1-68390-061-0
Printed in the United States of America

Theme Park Press | www.ThemeParkPress.com
Address queries to bob@themeparkpress.com

CONTENTS

Introduction v

Introduction

When I was four and a half, a guy in a mask tried to kidnap me. My parents did nothing. Well, nothing *useful*. Dad caught the whole thing on camera. One of those 80s, suitcase-sized numbers that barely fit on your shoulder, let alone in your pocket or purse. Meanwhile, I screamed bloody murder. Eventually, I resorted to self-defense, trying to knock loose my assailant's buck teeth, clawing his whiskered snout, grabbing an ear and yanking, then finally punching him in the nose. His big, round, rubber nose.

This did little to deter him, and I resigned to defeat in the form of a giant, death-squeeze hug. My world went black. When I opened my tear-filled eyes a few seconds later, he was gone. Dad was still rolling. Mom was straightening my Mickey ears. And I...well, I was hooked.

I dried my face on my sleeve, cracked a smile, and ran off to find my new best friend, giggling all the way. Until a five-foot duck, who I thought wanted to eat me, appeared out of nowhere, and I kind of freaked out again. But, the point is, I survived.

What's more, I watched the tape a hundred times when I got home. Begged my parents to take me back to that beautiful, nightmarish playground that stood a mere eighteen-hour mini-van ride away. Loved every minute of every trip down to Florida whenever they agreed. Dreamed of being a part of it all myself someday. And, when the chance came as a kid out of college with a wife and big dreams, but no real job prospects, I headed south and threw my lot in with the Mouse.

After all those years, I finally had a mask of my own. And since Mom and Dad, and the U.S.S. *Camcorder,* weren't there to capture all the screaming and crying and smiles and laughter this time, I figured I'd better write it down. This story. *My* story...of Mouse and men, of big, round, rubber noses, and, yes, even the occasional man-eating duck.

CHAPTER ONE

Training Week

When I was first hired—or "cast," to put it in Disney-speak—and learned that I'd been given the role of Goofy, I was absolutely thrilled. For obvious reasons. We're talking about one of Walt's own progeny, straight out of the golden days of Disney animation. Plus, ever since the big guy tried to accost me on that first trip to the Magic Kingdom, the two of us had shared a special bond. He was my absolute favorite growing up. I remember watching—and loving—everything he was in, and trying to imitate both what I saw and heard on-screen. This adoration led to the short-lived decision during my awkward chubby stage to be a stand-up comedian (a period I've nearly convinced myself, my parents, and my friends never existed, thanks to the fact that all photo evidence mysteriously wound up in a backyard bonfire).

The only time I ever went public with my act was around the kids' table at holiday gatherings. The laughs I received inspired a harmless amount of self-confidence—along with a steady stream of impressions (*hyucks* and *ah-hoo-hoo-hooeys* galore) that I'd perfected on my tape recorder back home (also invited to the bonfire). Luckily, my little cousins' enthusiasm was not such that it sustained the dream a day past puberty. My voice dropped two octaves, and my impressions went to hell. Plus, I'd just entered junior high school, and was suddenly subjected to a new set of rules in regard to acceptable social behavior and its implications for getting a girlfriend.

It's funny how I was so quick to abandon my comedic dreams to avoid an ass-kicking from my peers, and yet a few years later, strapped on floppy ears and size thirty-six shoes, and thought myself the dog's pajamas. The "Disney Difference," I guess.

Though I stopped flaunting my cartoon allegiances as a self-conscious middle-schooler, the love I held in my heart for Goofy and the Disney gang remained. I even hid the long-billed, dog-eared hat my grandmother had bought me on a childhood trip to the parks in a cardboard box at the top of my closet. Every now and then I'd pull it down, give it a good whiff to make sure the Disney World smell remained, and put it on to see if it still fit. It always did. Which is why, too-cool-for-school stage or not, I experienced a pretty emotional moment when I donned the actual costume for the very first time. A real full-circle kind of thing.

The twelve of us that made up our character training group—ten girls and two guys—were ushered into a large room, laid out like a dance studio. Bare floor, mirrors on the wall, stretching bar...you get the idea. The lot of us had spent the past three days in lectures, discussions, film screenings, and acting classes...and survived. Now, the moment we'd all been waiting for: the coronation, crowning, bestowing of head upon body. The eyes, ears, and faces of the greatest entertainment company in the world were about to become our own. It was like Halloween, Christmas, and Graduation Day all rolled into one.

Against the wall sat a line of smiling Disney character heads. The sight was somewhat unnerving, like stumbling into a Trader Sam-inspired horror flick or something. Odd, to say the least, when you've watched and laughed along with these iconic likenesses so many times since birth that you practically recognize them as family members. I'm not just talking about film and television, either. For someone who frequented the Disney parks as much as I did growing up, these were the faces on which I'd planted sloppy kisses as a toddler, posed for pictures beside, and shyly whispered autograph requests to.

"Weird." "Freaky." "Now, that's just wrong." Those were only a few of the comments from the group, as we huddled in the far corner of the room, as if maintaining our distance out of respect for the beheaded.

Once the shock wore off, and we began to inch closer, however, the adrenaline kicked in again.

"Go ahead. They don't bite," said the trainer.

The majority were mice and ducks. Only one dog in the bunch. Being the lone member north of six feet in height, I knew he was all mine.

We approached cautiously as a single line facing off against our new identities.

"We don't have all day," said the trainer, his patience wearing thin.

I took the plunge, kneeling and scooping up the head. I held it aloft in my hands like it was the Holy Grail. I may have imagined it, but I could have sworn for a second that the bland fluorescence of the room turned to a shimmering, almost blinding light, and a choir of Tinker Bells began to sing. The heavenly buzz of pixie wings was cut short, however, by my sinning mouth.

"Oh, shit," I said, nearly dropping the heavy noggin. I grabbed onto the big rubber nose and held on for dear life. *Solid son-of-a-bitch, aren't ya?*

Somewhere down the line, a Minnie-head crashed to the floor.

"Careful," scolded the trainer. "Heavier than they look."

The tiny girl at fault turned redder than the bow between her counterpart's mouse ears.

The trainer made his way down to me. "Heaviest one of all," he said giving the snout a pat.

"Great."

"It's the hat. Adds an extra ten pounds."

I turned the mask over in my hands a few times, getting a feel for its size and weight. The trademark stovepipe cap was permanently affixed. Coupled with the face's elongated snout, it gave the piece an awkward distribution.

I brought it close and sniffed. *No Disney World smell in there.* More like someone had dumped a cocktail of various bodily fluids inside, then spiked it with Windex.

Cries of pain from a couple of the group members interrupted my inspection.

"Owww! How are you supposed to..."

"What the hell? This thing is scalping me."

The trainer shook his head and went over to assist. He helped pull the mouse heads off two of his charges, untangled the hair of another. "Not so fast. You're skipping some steps."

First he chides us for being too standoffish, now for being too eager. He was definitely enjoying this.

He began handing out white, square pieces of fabric.

"I surrender," joked one of the girls, to whom his last comment had been directed, as she waved it overhead.

"Skull caps," he announced, holding one in the air.

"Ah, do-rags," corrected my buddy, the only other guy in the group. He placed it on his head.

"Exactly...step one," said the trainer.

We all followed suit. The white squares were much smaller than an actual handkerchief, and had thin ties on two corners.

A couple of the girls helped us guys secure them, tucking our hair under the edges.

We finished and collectively flashed a thumbs-up to our trainer, proud grins showing, as if we'd really accomplished something.

"What do you want? A turkey leg?" he said in response, trying not to smile at his own joke. He retrieved a box from the corner and dropped it in the middle of us. "Step two."

Inside lay a tangle of plastic.

I stepped forward to fish out whatever the hell "step two" was. I grabbed and pulled, and out came a line of the objects—all intertwined.

The trainer chimed in with his favorite word. "Careful."

I apologized and began sifting through the mess. What I ended up with looked and acted a lot like the guts of a construction helmet: the adjustable apparatus that keeps your head safe and secure within the harder plastic shell.

We all put them on and began sizing accordingly.

"Feel comfortable?" the trainer asked the girl next to me, after she'd finished.

"Yep."

"Then you're doing it wrong."

He explained the fit needed to be extra tight, in order to support the considerable weight of the masks.

We adjusted further, pulling tight enough to release a handful of yelps from those members with either low pain tolerances or fat heads.

My scalp tingled from the snug plastic. I looked around at my fellow trainees.

The girl next to me had a double fold in the skin between her eyebrows, due to the tightness.

My buddy winced as he struggled to rescue his ears, pulling them out from under the plastic. Once free, he began raising his eyebrows repeatedly, to be sure he still had mobility in his facial muscles. Each time, the line of circular indentations across the span of his forehead— red enough to be a permanent tattoo—peeked out from under the gray sizing band.

"Sucks," he said, struggling to move his mouth.

The trainer heard and sneered. "This is the easy part."

"What do you call this death trap?" the girl across from me asked.

"Headgear."

"Well, I hate headgear."

Once we'd all finally adjusted to not being able to feel the tops of our heads, we were told to take them off.

"Leave the sizing," the trainer explained, "and attach the headgear to the pegs inside your mask."

We retrieved our heads and followed orders.

"Third and final step."

My heartbeat quickened.

"When it's secure, go ahead and pull *it* and the mask over your head."

Moment of truth.

I tugged on the sizing strap to make sure there was no give, and prepared to enter. I would have taken a deep breath to play up the drama of the whole thing, but I thought it best to ingest as little stank as possible. I smiled as I slipped into my alter-ego.

The world went quiet and dark.

My head wobbled beneath the weight. Enough so, that I even stumbled slightly. But, when I found my balance, I stood taller than I had a few seconds earlier.

Oh, yes. I loved this. The way it felt. Not just on my head.

Despite having squirrelled all that Goofy-love away during middle and high school, it was still there. Alive and well. And it came flooding back at once. Lightening the load, lessening the odor, making my chest and the rest of my body tingle. In a good way. Not a *headgear* sort of way. Hell, yeah...still there.

Though no one could see me beaming (probably *because* no one could see me beaming), I kept doing so for the ten minutes we were given to acclimate to our new environments.

Some in the room grew claustrophobic and ripped their heads off almost immediately. "How are we s'posed to breathe in these things?"

"You're not. It's a sacrifice we make for the magic," replied the trainer, a smirk on his face.

The girl who'd asked put her mask back on, if only to cuss out the trainer without him knowing.

"Walk around. Get used to the limited visibility. It takes some time to..."

Crash. Two Mickeys collided and the crack of plastic echoed throughout the room.

The trainer's warning, this time, reached near-shouting level. "Care..."

"I know, I know," before he could finish. "Sorry."

Eventually, he herded us back into a line and put us through various motion exercises.

"Dance!"

The room sprung to life. I jumped out of the way to avoid a moonwalking Mickey. A Donald took it in the face after someone got carried away with their hip-to-sky disco points, a la *Saturday Night Fever*. I thought it safest to remain in one place, and so eased into a timid hula.

"Ride a surfboard!"

We quickly transitioned.

"Whooooooaaaaaahhhh," somebody said, as they pretended to catch a wave.

"No talking!" shouted the trainer.

The room fell silent, save for the subtle sounds of movement and accompanying panting.

"Pretend you're being chased by the Wicked Queen!" the trainer directed.

Our oversized heads bounced around the room, with our skinny little arms raised in terror. A mob of t-shirted bodies being dragged along for the ride made for a memorable view out the black-screened dog mouth: my new window to the world.

"Enough for today," said the trainer finally.

Beet-red faces emerged from the masks, as we all struggled to regain breath. Skull caps were pulled off and the sweat wrung out. Some around me were smiling, others recovering from what looked to be asthma attacks.

The trainer made his rounds with a pleased look on his face. "Not much oxygen in there."

I held the head admiringly, face-to-face, studying the design and detail: rubber whisker sprouts, buck-teeth, bulbous nose. I wiped a fingerprint smudge from the nose, and wondered how many kids had slobbered and drooled all over the thing.

The trainer strode up. "What do you think, Goof?"

"Yes," was all I could say. I looked him in the eye and smiled.

He nodded his approval, then called for everyone to meet him in the conference room across the hall in five minutes. "Full-body tomorrow," he promised, as he exited.

"Nice," said my buddy, setting his head down next to mine against the wall.

A couple girls groaned at the thought of costume additions, having already exceeded their perspiration limits for the year.

I was looking forward to it. I'd always been a sucker for Disney insider details and info, and this was about as behind-the-scenes as you could get. "Can't wait," I told him.

After a handful of lectures the next morning about topics like "Appropriate vs. Inappropriate Touching" and "What to Do If a Guest Pulls Your Tail," we got the news we'd be heading over to Epcot to suit up in full-costume. There was even a rumbling about the possibility of making an appearance in the park. In *public*. As in, guests.

I panicked momentarily when I heard, but figured there was no way we'd be going out already. We'd just gotten the feel of the mask the day before, and still hadn't even seen what the rest of our costumes entailed.

"He's just trying to scare us," I whispered to my buddy on the van ride over.

Arriving at our backstage location, we parked in front of an unassuming, modular-style building. Single file, we marched behind our trainer into a room that reminded me somewhat of my high-school locker room—minus the athlete's-foot smell and community showers. There were also a couple of large "showbiz" mirrors on either side of the room—the kind with the big round bulbs on all sides that made you feel as if you were in a starlet's dressing room in old Hollywood. In front of each locker lay a sizable and, by the looks, *heavy* bag. They rivaled some of my group members in size. They were made of thick cloth akin to an army rucksack, but were solid black and had long pull-ties to allow the carrier to tote it over her/his shoulder, like a Goth-version Santa Claus might.

The trainer started assigning lockers.

As each of our names was called, we assumed our places next to our big, black bags.

"Costumes were packed for you today," said the trainer. "First and last time that'll happen."

I nudged my bag with my shoe: it didn't budge.

"I'll be around to go through the different elements of each individual costume. Take a look and start unpacking while you wait for your turn."

I dove into the contents. On top was the now-familiar head. I laid it carefully on the ground and reached for the next item. Plain gray t-shirt. Boring.

Next up: plain gray t-shirt. *Umm...ok.*

And another...and another. *Hope I don't have to wear these all at once.*

The matching duds were followed by four pairs of identical black shorts.

"I have like eight changes of clothes in my bag," said the girl three lockers down.

"Your new wardrobe," said the trainer. "We call them *basics*."

"A uniform under a uniform," said my buddy, quietly enough that the trainer didn't hear. "Leave it to Disney."

Further inspection of the clothing revealed that neither shirts nor shorts—though one solid color—were *entirely* plain. Across the middle of the chest of each was a rectangular white tag sewn into the fabric. Each tag contained a barcode and sequence of random characters. The same could be found on the front leg of each pair of shorts.

"Are they gonna track us?" said a nearby girl in a low voice.

"That's some *Big Brother* shit," my buddy responded.

This time the trainer heard and sent an eye-roll our way. "It's for the laundry room's inventory."

"Sure it is."

"But why are there so many?" I asked.

"You'll see," was all he said back.

I continued rummaging and pulled out a pair of black tights, another pair—but for your arms—and an oversized pair of blue pants, complete with a big orange patch.

"Goofy's a hobo," I said, holding up my find.

"All those royalty checks, you'd assume he could afford clothes without holes in them," my buddy replied.

"Whatcha got?" I said to him, suddenly interested in the furry costume emerging from his black bag.

"It's a bear."

The girl on the opposite side of him looked and shouted, "Yogi!"

The entire room seemed to inhale together, in shock over the blasphemous comment. The trainer spoke as if he were addressing a life-and-death matter. "Yogi's. Not. Disney."

"Plus, Yogi's brown, not gray," added my buddy. He met my eyes and mouthed, "Dumbass."

As he pulled out his costume head, I started freaking out. "No way!"

"You know this guy?"

"Big Al!"

The Disney geeks around the room let out adoring sighs.

I began humming "Blood on the Saddle" as I returned to unpacking. I pulled out a pair of yellow suspenders, along with a matching vest, fuzzy orange shirt, and two brown leather shoes that rivaled the length of the arm with which I retrieved them from the depths of the bag. Next came a "beer gut," in the form of an under-vest with a belly-pad sewn on the front.

"A *fat* hobo," I said, turning again to my buddy and showing him my latest find.

Last, but not least, I brought forth the signature white gloves reserved for Disney royalty and tried them on for size.

"You ready?" said the trainer, eyeing my empty bag.

"Yep."

"Step behind the curtain and get into basics."

In the corner of the room was a strung piece of wire with a large piece of fabric draped over it. I ducked behind it and did as I was told.

"Tights are next," he said impatiently.

I rushed to follow orders, dressing like I was late for school. I put on both the leg and arm tights.

"Belly."

I strapped it on.

"Neck fur."

"Neck what?" I looked around the floor to try and locate what he meant.

He snatched up my bag and flipped it over. Out came what amounted to a cloak made of black fur—except the idea was to wear it in front, not back.

"What's this for?" I asked.

"The mask's got no neck, so you have to wear one." He said it like it was the most obvious thing in the world.

"Now, put the *clothes* on, just like a human would."

I laughed to myself at the oddity of this directive, then stepped into my pants, one leg at a time. I attached my suspenders to the oversized buttons on the front and back sides of my trousers, pulled on my fleece shirt, and topped it off with the vest.

I placed my feet in the floppy shoes, laced them up, and tried them out for a few steps. Doing so, I caught a glimpse of myself in one of the starlet mirrors and grinned at the sight. I represented the polar opposite of the day before: my oversized and exaggerated body all but swallowed up my little pinhead.

"You know what to do next," said the trainer, motioning toward a familiar-looking box in the middle of the room.

I retrieved skull cap and headgear, and set about squeezing my brains out.

"Head on," he ordered.

The room dimmed and a sort of peaceful silence enveloped me as I placed it on my shoulders.

That smile from the day earlier returned to my face.

I heard a muffled, "Turn around," issue from somewhere in the direction of the trainer.

I spun, and he checked that my neck fur was covering any and all trace of reality beneath the costume.

"And gloves," he said, apparently satisfied.

I bent down and almost ate the floor, not accounting for the extra weight on my head that was too busy obeying the laws of gravity to be bothered by a little thing like *my balance*. Luckily, my mile-long shoes were enough to keep me upright. On my second try, I bent at the knees, lowering myself, while keeping my head—and *his*—erect.

"Finished!" I said excitedly, as I pulled the second glove into place.

"Take it off and do it again," he said flatly. "This time, no help."

"OK."

"And practice keeping your mouth shut when you're in costume."

I raised my four-fingered glove and attempted a thumbs-up. Prohibited by the fat, padded fingers, it came out looking a little like a hang-loose sign.

"What the hell's that?" the trainer said smartly.

I changed my thumbs-up to a raised middle finger. He couldn't even tell.

Someone could, though. As the trainer moved on to assist another group member, I heard Big Al give a little chuckle off to my side.

I began to strip down to basics to start the whole process over. I watched amusedly as my training partners were slowly transformed into a most interesting cast of characters. There were, of course, the familiar faces—the mice, ducks, and dogs—but sprinkled throughout were another Country Bear or two and some more throwbacks I hadn't seen since childhood. The confusion that had surrounded Big Al's identity was repeated again and again, as more black bags emptied.

"Training groups get the leftovers," said the trainer, the fourth time he was questioned about a costume.

"Never seen this dog in my life," said one girl, suspiciously eyeing a Robin Hood head.

Another girl on the other side of the room had the same look on her face, as she stood there surveying the contents of her bag.

I strained to see around Big Al's house-size frame to confirm what I thought I'd seen, then headed over mid-change with an excited look on my face.

"Son!" I cried.

The girl looked behind her to see who I was talking to.

I bent down and gave the head on the ground next to her a fatherly pat.

She picked it up and tousled the sprigs of hair atop the mask. "You know this guy?"

"You *don't*?"

"Even I know who that is," Yogi-girl chimed in.

"*Goof Troop*?" I said.

Nothing.

"*A Goofy Movie?*"

Nothing.

I gave her my best P.J. impression in re-creating a scene from the film and started chanting, "Max! Max! Max! Max!"

A few others around me joined in, before the room broke into laughter.

By that time, the girl's face was bright red. "Nerds," she stated, before turning her back on us and continuing the process of changing.

"You should have to pass a test or something," I said quietly to Big Al, heading back over to my locker.

"Like Disney knowledge?"

"Definitely."

"Or maybe just an IQ test," he said, his giant, hairy belly bouncing up and down as he laughed at his own wit.

I joined in. Jokes just seemed funnier coming from a five-hundred-pound bear wearing a cowboy hat.

We overheard a fellow trainee, halfway into a Minnie costume, tell the girl beside her that she was crossing her fingers to play Dora the Explorer.

"Oooh, that'd be cool," said her friend.

Big Al shook like an earthquake.

I had to retreat behind the changing curtain just to compose myself.

Once I'd changed into my costume on my own a few more times—save the neck fur, which required the help of whoever wasn't wearing a mask or gloves at the time—the trainer approached and asked for an autograph.

"Who should I make it out to?" I joked.

He didn't laugh, but instead simply handed over an au-tograph book—the type sold throughout the resort (and

which sat, filled and stacked, in my Disney keepsake boxes back home).

Looking down through my black-screened window,
I flipped to a blank page and signed it no problem. Our
training group had spent a portion of each day the past
week focusing on autographs. We'd been given sheets of
paper with the official Disney-created signature of each
of the characters in our eligible height range.

"Memorize," said the trainer, upon handing them out.
"And practice, practice, practice."

"All of them?" complained one girl.

Instead of answering, the trainer just gave her one of
his trademark looks.

A few heavy sighs could be heard around the room.

"There will be a test," the trainer announced to more
sighing and complaining.

"My handwriting sucks," came a voice from the
peanut gallery.

The trainer quieted his voice in an attempt to convey
his seriousness. "And if you fail, you'll be outta here load-
ing logs on Splash Mountain before you can say *zip-a-
dee-doo-dah.*

The comment brought forth a few chuckles.

They were cut short almost immediately. "I'm serious."

The laughter ceased and the pen caps popped. The
twelve of us started signing until we had to ask for
more paper.

I already had Goofy's down pat. In fact, I'd started
practicing when I first received notification that I'd been
offered a position within the entertainment department.
As a character performer, your job title is determined by
your height range. When I'd gotten the initial offer of
employment, the position was listed on the form simply as Goofy Character Performer. Naturally, I thought
I would be exclusively "playing" Goofy in my new role
and immediately grabbed an old autograph book out of

my closet, traced over the Big Dog's signature, and set about perfecting it. I even threw on my winter gloves to try and mimic the feel of the oversized costume hands. After about three notebooks' worth of scribbling, I felt good and ready. It therefore came as a shock to learn that I'd be portraying *many* other characters, and be accountable for their signatures, as well.

There are more characters than one would think in the six-feet-plus height range, and I had my work cut out for me. Thankfully, my one-time stand-up comedian dreams as a child had been preceded by aspirations of becoming an animator, and I'd learned my way around a sketchbook. I'd also received a gold star in kindergarten penmanship, so I had that going for me. Still, the little Disney quirks integrated into the various signatures—Jafar's cobra head or Launchpad's propeller, for example—took some getting used to. It wasn't so much the difficulty of the material, but more so learning to bang out such a detailed autograph in a timely manner. It horrified me to think of some poor kid at the head of a mile-long line bawling for an autograph, while I stood there carefully putting on the finishing touches of Woody's Y-tail lasso like I was Audio-Animatronic Michelangelo in Spaceship Earth or something. Thankfully, the time spent in class, as well as the hours of scribbling that I put into the homework assignments each night, left me feeling good about my chances on the final exam.

Even so, I'd expected the test would be reserved for the final day of training—still a few days out—and so the trainer's request had caught me a bit off-guard.

"Perfect," said the trainer, as I handed over the signature.

I breathed a sigh of relief.

"One more time," he said, passing the book back.

I clicked the pen, but before I could sign, he gave further instructions.

"Arms up in the air," he said.

I complied.

"Higher."

I continued to raise them—autograph book still in hand—high enough that I might as well have been barreling down a hill on Expedition Everest.

"There ya go. Feel where your hands are?"

"Uh-huh."

"That's where your eyes are."

"My eyes?" I said, not understanding.

"Goofy's eyes...*your* eyes."

"OK."

"Did you look at the paper when you signed that autograph?" he asked.

"Well, yeah."

"But Goofy didn't."

"Shit," I said to myself, realizing finally what the trainer wanted from me. "So, I have to sign all the way up here?"

"Goofy can watch, but you can't."

I shook my head inside the mask. Book more than a foot above my head, I blindly struggled to even put pen to paper. The oversized gloves weren't helping. I lost a good grip and heard the pages of the book fan open. Now, I had no idea which pages were blank and which were already filled with signatures. I fumbled a bit more and dropped the pen. I began to lower my arms to retrieve it.

"I got it," the trainer said quickly. "Hands up," he directed.

He placed the pen back in my hands, and I managed to hold on long enough to sign.

"Let's see," said the trainer, whipping the book out of my hands. "Not bad."

I started to grin, until he shoved the finished product in front of Goofy's mouth-hole, and I realized he was being sarcastic.

Several of the pages were bent and crinkled from my awkward handling of the book. In worse shape still was my signature. I'd basically written all five letters of Goofy's name in the same place—one on top of the other—rendering nothing more than a scribbled mess. About an inch-and-a-half above the chicken-scratch was the *underline* which was, of course, supposed to run *below* the signature.

Unable to look at the abomination a second longer, I reached forward to close the book. Doing so, I saw that my left-hand glove—moments ago, pristine and fresh off the costuming rack—was scarred by several ink lines from my shaky effort. I lowered my arm immediately and tried to nonchalantly hide it behind my back.

"Don't worry about it," the trainer said, much to my relief. "It's only a mild case," he said, nodding toward the marked hand.

I raised it to inspect the damage.

"Character Glove," he said. "That's what we call it."

I began to feel a little better about myself.

"Everyone comes down with it by the end of a shift," he explained, with only a hint of a smile on his face. "The good news," he said, turning to Big Al and low-fiving his furry paw, "is that bears can't get it."

He turned and eyed Mickey and Minnie. "Mice usually get hit hardest."

The pair shuddered, as if it were an actual disease.

"That's what bleach is for," the trainer said, tossing me the autograph book.

It bounced off my belly pad and into my cumbersome hands.

"You've got work to do."

I nodded.

"And only twenty minutes to do it in."

Surprised, I raised my head to look him in the eye through the black screen, which meant Goofy became suddenly fixated on the fluorescent light bar directly overhead. "What do you mean?"

"We're going out," he announced.

The room froze. All eyes turned to the trainer.

"You heard me."

Big Al started pumping his first Arsenio Hall-style.

All I could do was think about my bumbling autograph attempt. "But the test…" I said. "We haven't taken it yet."

"Pop quiz," he said with an evil grin.

All around the room, trainees started scrambling to find writing utensils and any blank writing surfaces.

Big Al, however, remained calm, save the celebratory jig he'd launched into.

I was a little perturbed that my buddy was so happy, while I was panicking. "What are you so excited about?"

"I'm going to Disney World," he shouted through his mask.

I couldn't help but crack a smile.

"What about your autograph, jackass?"

"My eyes aren't half-a-mile over my head, ya freak," he responded, still shouting to ensure he was heard through the fur.

I looked around and noticed that everyone else's signing positions were relatively normal. Big Al was right: I was the freak, the only one in the bunch who had to figure out how to sign completely blind.

I clenched my jaw, raised my hands to the ceiling, and tried again. I brought it down for a look and saw that I'd managed to fit *G-o-o* on the page before running out of room. Where the *f* and *y* ended up, I'll never know. Probably on my glove.

I gave it another go: this time the name was at least legible, but the full length of the *underline* had been done on my left thumb, rather than the page.

After several more attempts and as many failures, I turned to Big Al, who was churning out exemplary autographs left and right. "Got any whiskey in that saddle-bag of yours?"

"Still sucking?" he said, without an ounce of sympathy.

"You've got it bad," said a Daisy Duck who was passing by.

"What?"

"Character Glove," she said, grabbing my left hand and surveying the damage.

"Lemme write you a prescription for that," Big Al chimed in, his belly beginning to shake, as he scribbled effortlessly onto his pad of paper, ripped the page out, and plastered it against the mouth-hole of my mask.

Try Universal, said the flawless handwriting.

Before I could start beating the crap out of Big Al, the trainer's cry—"Five minutes!"—set the room abuzz and me back to practicing.

Another few mangled autographs in, my concentration was broken by a parade of newcomers into the dressing room. Four girls dressed in blue button-up shirts and khaki shorts, along with an older heavyset man sporting the same outfit, entered in a single-file line.

"Characters," announced our trainer, demanding the room's attention. "Meet your attendants."

They smiled and waved, and began looking around the room, seemingly fascinated by the costumed chaos around them.

"They'll be your eyes and ears out there," the trainer continued. "And, it should go without saying, your *mouths*. Understood? You talk, you're gone."

We all knew him well enough by that point to refrain from answering, and the lot of us all merely shook our heads in agreement or gave a thumbs-up.

"Exactly," he said, looking pleased.

He began making his way around the room, stopping briefly at each locker to inspect the autograph-work being produced.

I raced to get a few more practice runs in.

He saved me for last, and when he finally approached, he did so very slowly.

I'm not sure if he was trying to make me more nervous or allow me a little more practice time. Regardless, he was upon me in no time, moment-of-truth look on his face.

I took a deep breath, raised my hands in prayer—I mean, the air—and tried my best to channel that tiny, wannabe animator self that I hoped was still living somewhere deep inside. I crawled my way through the signature—the loop of the *G*, double-*o*, backwards-*f*, tail of the *y*—and steadied myself for the *underline*. My Achilles heel. I moved my pen ever so slightly downward to where I guessed the bottom of my letters reached, held my breath, and...let 'er rip. The pen-stroke felt good—clean. I was pretty sure I hadn't caught any glove fabric. It felt like all page to me. I slowly lowered the book, and without looking, handed it over to the trainer.

He studied it for a moment, then said flatly, "You spelled it wrong."

My head fell, meaning Goofy was now looking my trainer in the eyes, rather than me.

The trainer slid the autograph book under the mouth-hole. "Just kidding," he said with a chuckle.

I looked at the page and, by some sort of miracle, could actually read the name before me. I erupted in silent celebration inside my mask and raised my inked left fist in triumph.

In solidarity, Big Al started in with his jig once more.

"Proud of ya, dad," shouted Max from across the room.

Pluto bounded up to give me a fake tongue-lick.

I high-fived a couple of ducks. In doing so, the trainer noticed my nearly all-black left glove.

"Time to amputate," he said. He located an extra and instructed me to swap mine out. "And fast," he said. "You're on, Goof!"

CHAPTER TWO

Into the Wild

Our training group lined up at the dressing room exit, as our trainer, along with the squad of attendants, gave us one last look-over for any costume malfunctions.

"Remember your signals," our fearless leader ordered, as if he was prepping his troops for battle.

During the past week, we'd learned various hand signals that could be used to communicate "onstage" with character attendants, once our mouths were bound and gagged by the Disney magic. The only one of any import was the SOS sign, which signaled to cast members around you that something was wrong and you needed to exit to a backstage area immediately. We were instructed only to use it in emergency situations, meaning you were about to pass out or your mask was about to fill with vomit. The sign was made by placing your left hand over the character's left eye and raising your right hand in the air. We'd all been using it jokingly ever since we'd learned it.

For instance, if the trainer asked us a question in class and we didn't know the answer, we'd simply raise the signal to acknowledge our surrender. Or, when one of our mice showed up for training one morning with a bit of a hangover, and looking like hell, we asked her how she felt, and without a word: eye covered, hand up. In fact, I'd used it only minutes earlier when Robin Hood had strolled up and inquired about my autograph progress.

Once we received the OK from our costume inspectors, and I'd had my neck fur tucked and tightened one last time, we began to march. I gave myself a last glance in the dressing room mirror on our way out. *Not bad*, I thought to myself, as I bobbed on by.

The second my boat shoes stepped into that Florida sunshine, my entire mask flooded with humidity, and I gasped for any last trace of air-conditioned oxygen before it turned to steam. I felt a bead of sweat start down my nose. *Already?* It started to tickle as it inched downward, and I raised my arm to wipe it with my sleeve. My shoulder was stopped a good eight inches away from making contact by a long, whiskered snout: my *other* nose. Another bead rolled down and combined forces with the one already there. It was now a full-on droplet. My nose was itching like crazy. I shoved a white glove in and out of Goofy's mouth, trying to push the view screen in far enough to brush against my nose and relieve the maddening sensation. No such luck. I began to panic. I looked around me, not recognizing any of my surroundings. I had to do something, go somewhere to take care of the itch. I wanted to rip my nose from my face—right after I ripped my dog head off my body.

"Feeling good?" my trainer call from the front of the line.

I wanted so badly to speak up, but I was too ashamed. We'd been out of the dressing room all of thirty seconds. Out of the corner of my screen, I suddenly saw a flash of blue. I turned to the khaki-clad attendant herding us onward and grabbed her arm.

She let out a small shriek of terror from the shock of being accosted, out of nowhere, by an eight-foot dog.

I pulled her in as close as possible and whispered, "Blow in my mouth."

She looked at me dumbfounded.

I repeated my plea for help, raised a white glove to my eye screen, and pointed out the target area. "Please, just do it."

"Excuse me?"

"BLOW. IN. MY. MOUTH."

She made an I-hate-you face, took a deep breath, and let loose a tuna-wrap-flavored (courtesy of the cast cafeteria) gust that would have doused the candles on a birthday cake.

The puddle of sweat on the end of my nose dispersed like a popped water balloon. *Halle-friggin'-lujah.*

I gave my attendant-savior a pat on the back and continued marching. As we went, I watched my giant, familiar shadow keep time beside me, and chuckled to myself that it indeed belonged to me.

Soon, Asian-style architecture came into view above the tops of the buildings to our left. *Japan!* Finally, I had my bearings. We walked a few minutes more before coming to a stop at a white fence with a full-length mirror and reminder to cast members not to pass unless "show-ready." Also posted were several large warning signs, indicating that an "onstage" environment was mere steps away.

This is it! I said to myself, my heart beginning to race.

Our trainer brought us into a tight huddle—well, as tight as possible considering some of us were wearing costumes the size of small countries. "I'm going to number you, one through twelve. Don't forget your number!"

He started with me and worked his way around the circle. "You know what's on the other side of this fence?" he asked.

"Disney World?" said Big Al.

"Uh-huh. What else?"

"People," gulped Max.

"*Guests,*" corrected the trainer. "Lots and lots of 'em. And tape."

"Huh?"

"Numbered pieces of tape on the ground. I want you to find your number and plant yourself. No roaming, do you understand? Let the guests come to you."

We all nodded our understanding of his orders.

"Fifteen minutes. That's all you have to endure. We're in and out," he said.

He and the character-attendant trainer assigned each of the four girls to a group of three characters.

Tuna Breath got placed with me. She rolled her eyes when given the assignment.

"You are responsible for your characters," their trainer reminded them. "If anything happens to them out there, it's on you."

"Got it," they replied, as they switched on the walkie-talkies hanging from their belts.

"Alright, here we go!" said our trainer.

"Should we put our hands in and do a cheer?" asked Donald.

Big Al's head dropped. "Oh my god."

The rest of the group loved the idea.

"Disney, on three," said Donald.

All gloves, paws, and feathers extended, we shout-whispered our battle cry, due to the proximity of onstage, and broke the huddle.

One by one, we rounded the corner of the staggered entryway, designed to prevent guests from seeing backstage, and made our way to our very first set location as Disney character performers...the *restroom*?

Well, not exactly, but it might as well have been. Our strips of tape were positioned in a line, with some landscaping running along our backs, and the American Adventure's bathroom facilities a few yards ahead.

We all located our numbers on the ground. Our attendants stood a few feet off to guard us from...well, nobody. There wasn't a soul in sight.

Our trainer placed himself a considerable distance away, in order to observe the line as a whole.

The twelve of us swayed back and forth, shuffled our feet, or grooved to the music in our heads, the nervous energy not letting anyone stay still. The anticipation only grew as we continued to stand there unnoticed, tucked away from the busy thoroughfare, which lay fifteen yards out.

Eventually, our trainer started toward us. He didn't seem bothered that there were no guests around, but there was still a bit of urgency in his step.

He began heading straight for me, and I frantically checked myself on what I could possibly be doing wrong. I started feeling around my costume. Was my neck fur on straight? Ears tangled? Belly pad off-center?

"You're going fishin', Goof," he said matter-of-factly, as he approached.

"I raised my hands and shrugged my shoulders to indicate I hadn't the slightest idea of what he was talking about."

"Get out there and start reelin' 'em in," he said, giving me a little nudge toward the guest traffic.

I gulped and started forward, scuffing my shoe on the pavement and tripping slightly as I went.

"There ya go, Goof," said the trainer, thinking the stumble part of my act.

The compliment gave me a shot of confidence. I stuck out my belly pad, grabbed the belt of my trousers, and pulled them up emphatically in true Goofy fashion.

I looked over to see Big Al nodding enthusiastically at my performance.

I began to raise my knees high into the air as I walked, and planted each step of my enormous shoes extra hard into the pavement to make for an especially loud and awkward gait.

The mice were silently applauding with their poofy white gloves.

I continued to make my way down the line of my fellow trainees and toward the guests, hamming it up more and more with each step.

They spurred me on with some fist bumps and high fives. Robin Hood was "raising the roof" as I passed. Last in line was my son, Max. He gave me a you-da-man point.

The smile inside my mask evaporated as I suddenly found myself smack-dab in the middle of the street—alone, exposed, and unsure of what to do next. I closed my eyes and calmed my breathing. *You've been trained for this. You ARE Goofy.* I felt a pain in my right foot and a tightness in my leg. I opened my eyes and looked down to see a young boy—about three years old—wrapped around my right calf, standing on my shoe. He was holding on for dear life, while his brother and parents watched with giant smiles on their faces.

The dad began snapping pictures, and the mom began cooing over the cuteness of the moment. The brother jumped forward and latched onto my other leg. I looked around. Guests were descending on me from all sides—cameras out, autograph books extended. I knew I had to move fast. I reached down and took both boys by the hands. I started skipping back toward my line of friends, and the two of them soon joined in. I heard what sounded like ten or twenty more kids follow suit and start skipping behind us. I proudly led the crowd back to our little corner and the outstretched arms of a whole cast of characters waiting to show them some Disney lovin'. *Oohs* and *aahs* went up from countless guests scarcely able to believe their good fortune in happening upon a dozen characters without a single line.

I hurried my way over to my tape and set up shop. I tousled the hair of both little boys I'd brought with me, then knelt and gave them a nice, long hug.

Their mother had tears in her eyes, and the dad hadn't stopped clicking pictures since they'd first spotted me.

After a few more moments of affection, the mom stepped forward with a request. "Would you mind signing the boys' autograph book? They're too shy to ask."

Thank god—only one book. I nodded so hard my ears flapped up and down, then raised the book to "eye-level" and hoped for the best.

Maybe it was the excitement of my first family, or some good ol' fashioned Disney magic—possibly a delusion from the extreme heat—but I swear I've never seen a more perfect autograph than the one I handed over to those boys. Whether it was or not, the boys' eyes indicated they were more than pleased. They gave a couple last high-fives before making a beeline for Big Al.

Our trainer, who'd observed the interaction, was close on their heels, wearing as big a smile as I'd seen from him all week. "You're a rock star, Goof," he said with a wink.

I knew it was true. I snapped my suspenders and wrapped my next family in a giant bear—err, *dog*—hug.

Our fifteen minutes flew by. Following our first showing in the park, the dressing room was like a locker room after a Super Bowl win. We yanked off our heads to reveal giant smiles—and soaked skull caps—and began chatting a mile a minute about our experiences, as we changed back into street clothes.

Mask off, I rubbed my nose raw for a solid minute. It felt good to get Goofy's very warm set of clothes off. The tights on both my arms and legs had to be peeled off, as they'd been pasted to my skin with salty glue. My gray basics tee had turned black to match my shorts, thanks to the pool of sweat consuming its every fiber. The shorts themselves were embarrassingly wet as well, as if they were a pair of used swimming trunks. My underwear might as well have been *made* of liquid, and I opted to go commando once I'd changed, for fear of their wetness bleeding through my dry clothes. It was only when I'd gotten back into my street clothes and saw my bright red face in the starlet mirror that I realized how exhausted I was. If the atmosphere around me was that of a celebratory locker room, my body sure felt as if it'd been through a hard-fought game. A small pounding began in my head—the kind that shows up after you've been hotter than hell and used up in every way.

From the corner of the room, our trainer spoke. "Best part of the job…" he said, stepping aside to reveal a minifridge, "free Power-Ade."

He swung the door open to reveal loads of the blue-colored variety, as the entire room headed his way.

"Can't be picky. Disney only buys one flavor," he said, beginning to distribute the bottles.

Seeing my face as I took two bottles reminded him of something, and he spoke again. "You MUST remember to hydrate," he warned. "The heat, the movement, the adrenaline—it's going to take awhile to acclimate."

I chugged one bottle and started in on my second.

"Don't stop drinking. Ever." He handed out the last of the drinks and closed the mini-fridge.

"Words I live by," said a headless Big Al.

After a more formal recap of our first foray onstage, we were dismissed for the day. I headed straight home, popped two ibuprofen, and collapsed on the bed. I fell asleep to the rhythm of the pounding of my head before dinner-time and didn't wake until the next morning. When I did, I was spread-eagle on top of the covers, in the exact position I'd been when I laid down the night before. I couldn't believe how much those fifteen minutes of performing had taken out of me. And I considered myself in good shape. I jogged fairly regularly and, at the time, adhered to a strict vegan diet. Maybe that's why I was absolutely wrecked. Still, thinking back to the previous day, I realized I'd overdone it, even for such a short period of time. Skipping around in the heat of the sun and costume—which added a considerable amount of weight. Not to mention, kneeling, hugging, standing, dancing, kneeling again, playing peek-a-boo, hugging again, standing again, dancing again—you get the idea—at somewhat of a chaotic pace for a straight fifteen minutes without really stopping to take a breath had proven to be a workout the likes of which I hadn't experienced.

Sitting there, shoving toast into my mouth at the breakfast table as I loaded up on carbs and faced yet another day of training—no doubt a second, longer park appearance—I questioned whether I could handle the job. The longer I sat there, the more I talked myself out of it. I started getting tired just thinking about donning that costume again. I wondered out loud to my wife about a possible solution. Maybe I belonged at a Mickey Bar cart beneath a big ol' shade tree at the Animal Kingdom, I told her, or sweeping trash at a nice, slow pace on Main Street. Perhaps I'd be better off surrounded by a million gallons of cool ocean water at the Seas in Epcot, or shooting at mobsters and cowboys in the Great Movie Ride, rather than kissing and hugging tourists in the blistering sun. I found myself chickening out. We discussed who I might be able to call to request a transfer. But, I only had—I looked at the clock on the microwave—three minutes before I needed to leave. It'd have to wait until tomorrow. I downed a couple more ibuprofen, along with three full glasses of water—trying to rehydrate my system—said my goodbyes, and headed out the door.

By the time I unlocked my car, I had to pee. *Ah, screw it. A bursting bladder and aching kidneys while I squirm in I-4 traffic is probably as comfortable as I'm gonna get today. Might as well enjoy it.*

Thankfully, the first half of the training day consisted of a few various seminars and an indoor training session sans costumes.

After a video presentation meant to demonstrate the many mannerisms and styles of movements of various Disney animated characters, our trainer pushed the

TV cart back to the corner of the room and flipped on the lights.

The twelve of us sat cross-legged on the floor of the dance-studio-style room awaiting instructions.

"You've gotten a taste of the parks now," he said. "I liked what I saw..."

We began to smile, proud of yesterday's showing.

"For the most part," he finished, his voice turning slightly sharper. "Donald..." he pointed to the tiny twenty-something girl who'd portrayed the world's most famous duck the day prior, "Wave to me...right now."

She raised her hand, palm facing him, and flapped her four fingers up and down in place.

"That's a very ladylike wave you've got there," he said.

She started to thank him for the compliment, but was interrupted.

"Is Donald a girl or boy?" he asked impatiently.

She bowed her head in shame.

"Goof, wave for me."

I gave him a full-arm, side-to-side number.

"Boy wave," he said, pointing to me. "Girl wave," he said, pointing back to Donald.

We nodded that we understood.

"Mickey!" he roared, just getting going. "Also a boy." He went and stood next to yesterday's main mouse. "What's this?" he said, placing one foot toe-down on the ground behind him and thrusting his opposite arm dramatically forward like a figure skater.

"Uh...I never did that," the girl said, defensively.

"Uh...whenever a camera clicked," he shot back.

Her face turned red.

"Big Al," the trainer said, apparently not done making his point. "Stand up...lemme take a picture."

My buddy rose to his feet.

"One...two...three," the trainer counted before he snapped his fake camera.

Big Al struck a very unassuming pose—left arm out and a slight lean-in toward the camera and his invisible guest.

"Looks about right for an obese male bear, doesn't it?" he asked the rest of the group.

We gave Big Al a nice round of applause.

Before he could take his seat, however, the trainer continued. "OK, now you're Clarabelle Cow, and I wanna take your picture." Without any hesitation, he raised his fake camera and began quickly counting down.

In a fit of confusion, my friend attempted to strike the extra-feminine pose that the trainer had just called Mickey out for. He ended up looking ridiculous—like a ballerina awkwardly frozen in mid-glide—and the group let him know it with snickers and a few comments.

"Time for sex-ed," the trainer announced, bringing us to our feet.

Under his orders, we formed a single-file line at the back of the room.

He proceeded to call us forward one at a time, assign us a character to imitate—of the opposite sex, of course—and then critique us as we paraded around the open floor space in endless circles, mimicking the character's walk and various interactive elements—posing for pictures, waving, dancing, laughing, etc.

"Minnie Mouse," he called out, when it was my turn.

I started prancing around on my toes, trying to imitate—in an exaggerated way—what I thought walking in heels looked like. I raised both hands and pretended to smooth my hair. Laughed daintily with one hand in front of my mouth. Curtsied. Spun around in my imaginary dress. Kicked my heel back and leaned into the fake camera with pouty lips, like Marilyn Monroe.

I heard quite a bit of laughter coming from the back of the room. I didn't know which was worse: this or the parks.

Finally, after what seemed like miles of laps around the room making a fool of myself, the trainer moved on to the next in line.

My only consolation was my buddy's performance.

The trainer tried to be nice and stuck with the Clarabelle persona, but it didn't seem to help.

My friend—the only other *guy* in the group—followed my lead and attempted a sexy-ish, high-heels strut around the room, apparently forgetting Clarabelle has hooves only, no shoes. He then launched into all-out ballerina mode, prancing around on one leg, attempting shaky, off-balance twirls and spins.

The trainer put him out of his misery, when my friend braved a picture-pose pantomime that involved adjusting his invisible udders. "OK, OK," the trainer said, waving his hands to stop my friend. "Not that kinda sex-ed."

The room erupted into laughter.

My friend started to take a bow, then thought better of it, and gave us all a sweet, little curtsy.

Returning to the line, I gave him a manly fist bump. "We nailed that," I told him.

"Totally."

The girls around us were giggling, and I heard one of them say, "Now we know."

My friend and I asked what they meant.

"Oh, nothing," they replied, continuing to giggle.

"Come on," I coaxed.

"We were all wondering," piped up the girl next to me, "if you two were...ya know..."

"Since *every* guy in Entertainment is," added another.

"But now we know...*not* gay."

The two of us started laughing, but then realized they were all knocking the performances we'd just given.

"Hey, I could be gay if I wanted," said my friend, defending himself.

"Me too!" I chimed in.

They rolled their eyes and shook their heads, then launched into a hurtful parody of the dance moves we'd exhibited during the exercise.

"Alright," I admitted. "You coulda just asked what my colors were; that woulda told you right off."

My buddy started laughing and nodding his head knowingly. "Mm-hmm," he said, pointing to himself.

Disney's entertainment division determines an individual's dance and movement skill levels by a color-coded classification system. During initial auditions, a manager walks around taking notes while everyone is made to participate in a choreographed dance routine, as well as various role-playing and movement exercises. If you end up getting the job, you're assigned a color both for your dance abilities and your movement abilities, which then determines what specific character roles you're eligible to perform. I didn't score the lowest colors possible on either category, but certainly nowhere near *gay* level.

I remember at my first audition—which didn't take place on Disney property, but at a local dance studio near my hometown—I was nervous as hell. A few times a year, Disney sends a team from Entertainment on an audition tour around the country, stopping at various cities to recruit new talent. I don't think I'd ever been to an audition—of any kind—up to that point, and certainly not one that required any sort of dancing.

I grew up with somewhat of a musical background—listened to the stuff constantly, played a couple instruments, even formed a rock band with my buddies. But the extent of my dance experience was pretty much limited to the old *Dance Dance Revolution* video game. The only time I'd danced publicly was at a wedding when I was thirteen, and then only because the bride—an old family friend—forced me to. And only for half a song.

Though many straight males wouldn't consider themselves dance aficionados, I felt as if I had even less experience than the average guy. Most young men get to at least cut their teeth on middle and high school dances—homecoming, prom, maybe even a Sadie Hawkins if they're lucky. Unfortunately (for more reasons than just dance exposure), I was forced by my parents to attend a Christian school, all the way through to graduation, which meant no real male-female contact of any kind was tolerated—certainly not the heathen, teenage dance rituals of the day, or as our principal used to refer to it: sex with clothes on. So, while the rest of America was getting down on prom night, our senior class attended an elegant "banquet," complete with dinner, non-spiked punch, and some light praise-and-worship in the background.

While I didn't subscribe to the dance-is-from-the-devil mindset, I simply wasn't afforded any opportunity to hone my skills—thus, rendering me wholly unprepared the day I walked into my Disney audition and was given a minute's worth of choreography from *High School Musical* to learn and perform on the spot. The whole idea of blending into the crowd and hoping to stay unnoticed was a no-go, considering I was a foot-and-a-half taller than nearly everyone else in the room. All the tiny would-be mice and ducks were practically consumed by my towering dog shadow.

The choreographer seemed to be speaking a foreign language: grapevines, heel-toe combos, jazz hands. I was missing steps left and right, and finally resolved that my best strategy would be simply to smile—big, bold, and toothy—throughout the routine, whether I hit the choreography or not. I figured Disney was all about the smiles, and having fun with whatever it is you're doing, so I tried my best to grin and bear it—literally.

The dance portion of the audition finally over, I knew if I had any chance at all of working in Entertainment, I'd have to nail the second color-code assessment, which was the role-playing and movement audition. While I was absolutely certain that my scores on the first portion had been abysmal, I tried my best to put aside the fact that I'd brought shame upon the name of Troy Bolton, temporarily table the humiliation of what amounted to my debut on the dance floor, and make a somewhat decent showing in round two.

Each of the participants in the room were spotlighted and told to portray their favorite Disney character in pantomime until the rest of the room was able to guess who they were. I took the easy road and began to play-sword-fight, stopping intermittently to curl my mustache or brandish my hook.

"Captain Hook!" the group shouted not long after I'd begun.

Phew. I sheathed my sword and retreated.

"Too easy," said one of the managers. "Pick another."

Shit. I searched my brain for another character and landed on an equally-masculine choice. I must have been feeling pretty insecure about my lack of dance abilities, and been trying to convince myself and the judges that what I lacked in performance skills, I could make up for in manly traits like sword-fighting, or muscles, or height.

I flexed my biceps dramatically and struck a few body-builder-type poses. I picked up an invisible boulder and began to spin it around on one finger like a basketball, before tossing it aside and dusting off my hands like it'd been the easiest thing in the world.

Cries of "Hercules!" rang out from my audience of fellow auditioners.

Still in character, I smiled a big cheesy grin, worthy of a Greek god, and took an obnoxious bow. Thankfully, the managers let me off the hook and called out the next name on the list.

After a few more similar tests, the scores were tallied, and though I wouldn't know until a few weeks later that I'd at least clawed my way up a few notches on the performance color chart, I didn't figure my "herculean" efforts had been enough—after my dancing display—to secure my spot within the entertainment department.

Leaving the studio after the audition, a fellow participant approached. We had stood in line together earlier, where she'd shared that her second-choice role—like mine—was Attractions. The employment application had required you to select a few different options, and the two of us had concluded, while waiting for our names to be called during the movement exercise, that should we not make the cut, Adventureland Attractions would be our preferred consolation.

"Good luck," she said as we bumped into one another again exiting the studio.

Despite towering over her and the rest of the participants, I walked out those doors feeling a little shorter after my somewhat embarrassing efforts. I tried to force a smile and responded with a comment that summed up my assessment of how the day had gone. "See ya in the Tiki Room."

Needless to say, I was shocked to receive the congratulatory email a few weeks later, informing me of my new role as a character performer. I started feeling pretty good about myself, thinking that I must have really impressed the managers with my role-playing routines. But then, I spied a line in the email saying something about being assigned the specific role of Goofy, based on my height. *Ah, that explains it.* Thankfully, I thought to myself, in the performance world, I was a giant. Not for talent, skill, or experience—literally, just a giant. *Good enough for me.* Sure, I wasn't *gay*-good. Hell, not even really *straight*-good. But I was tall. And I was in.

On a side note, I ended up seeing the girl I'd talked with in line, about two years later. I was enjoying the parks on my day off, and she was waking up Josè with a stick, to kick off one of many of that day's shows in, you guessed it, Walt Disney's Enchanted Tiki Room. I felt awkward and kind of bad that I'd made it into Entertainment, and she hadn't. I didn't want to make her feel worse about herself or her job cleaning up animatronic bird poop by having a conversation, so I lowered my head when she passed by, in hopes that she wouldn't recognize me. She didn't, and I left without ever uttering a word.

All of that to say, back in the training room, so many weeks later, my buddy and I were able—thanks to our ineptitude, when it came to dance and performance—to set the record straight for our fellow trainees about our sexual orientation.

Once we'd gotten that out of the way, the group was ushered out to a fifteen-passenger character-mobile bound for backstage Epcot and our second go at in-park performance.

"Epcot again?" complained one of the girls on the way over.

"Least amount of guests this time of day," replied the trainer, as he dared her to say more by staring her down in the rearview mirror.

She took the bait. "I don't know what you're talking about; I'm ready. My Robin Hood was flawless yesterday."

"Well, besides the fact that you pointed your bow-and-arrow at three guests' faces and knocked over a toddler with your tail when you bent over to sign an autograph…"

The girl continued to defend herself. "But, did you *see* that autograph?" she said.

"Well, how are you with Scrooge's?"

"No problem," she said defiantly, though she began subtly unzipping her backpack to retrieve her autograph study sheets.

"Congratulations, you're an uncle," he said, watching her lay tracing paper and begin to work.

"Are we all switching it up?" asked my buddy.

"Only some."

My eyebrows raised hopefully, wondering if I'd be shedding my heavy-hatted burden for something easier, maybe less hot, too. I leaned forward to ask.

"Not you, Goof."

I slumped back down in my seat without ever getting a word out.

We soon pulled up to the same modular we'd been in the day before and were led into the familiar dressing room.

I grabbed a Power-Ade out of the fridge first thing.

A new load of black bags dotted the space in front of the lockers, and the twelve of us began the transformation process. About half the costumes were new, and so required a brief tutorial and some assistance by the trainer. Those of us with the same costumes as the day before were told to dress, undress, and dress again for practice.

I began to pace myself even while I changed. I took it nice and slow, following up each additional clothing item with an extra-large swig of Power-Ade. As I tied the skull cap around my head in preparation for the mask, I realized my neck muscles were incredibly sore. The weighty head didn't deserve all the blame. To look any guest in the eye—dog-to-human—I had to be peering straight down at the pavement with my *own* eyes. The awkward and uncomfortable position, compounded by the weight on top, had resulted in a painful stiffness that began to rear its ugly head as I prepared to put my other head on.

"Thirty-minute set this time," the trainer announced, as the moment of truth drew near.

"Same spot?" someone asked.

"Nah," said the trainer. "I feel like going to Canada today."

And so we did.

I'd like to say that my neck pain eased, sweat dripped to a stop, the tightness in my calf muscles—from a week of prancing, dancing, kneeling, and standing—subsided, and my energy and enthusiasm were rejuvenated by an overwhelming dose of Disney magic, as a crowd of World Showcase tourists gathered around for a piece of me. But I can't. Still, I didn't die in that dog costume. I'd even go so far as to say I made progress.

I started picking up on some tricks of the trade. If I spied a few young guests in line, I'd make my way down to one knee, and then stay there for two or three families in a row before standing again. If a moment called for dancing, I'd plant my feet and let my hips do the work, to conserve energy. The biggest thing was that I kept breathing. The day before, I'd been so enamored with the thrill of being in costume out in public for the first time, my heart had nearly beat out of my chest; I'd been racing around, wide-eyed, head spinning, out of breath for the whole set. It could have just been the pre-emptive ibuprofen I'd popped beforehand, but once the thirty minutes was up, I had only a mild headache. The most energy I exerted the whole set was self-inflicted, as I danced around to prevent peeing my pants, after pushing the fluids all day.

I felt more comfortable with my interactions, too. I started getting used to burying my head into my chest—triple-chin style—and straining my eyes as far upward as they'd go, in order to see out of Goofy's mouth-hole and achieve the desired mask placement for character eye contact. I picked up a few new moves: the *Aww-Shyucks-Ear-Twist*—like a timid little girl twirling a ringlet of hair with her finger, but with my long, floppy dog ear and big, white glove instead—which never failed to elicit a whimper from a sentimental mother watching her own shy young daughter meet Goofy for the first time, and the *Hiya-Sport-Noogie*, which was perfect for bratty and hyperactive pre-teen boys who were in need of a Disney-approved calming down.

The set didn't go perfectly, but my hope and faith were restored. I saw a light at the end of the tunnel, and started to believe once more that I could do the job. I figured I'd probably been a little over-dramatic and could shelve the idea—at least for the time being—of putting in for a transfer. Even my autograph was improving. I'd say about 90% of them had been legible, and I finished the half-hour with only a small case of Character Glove.

The highlight of the set, however, came as a result of one of my fellow trainee's penmanship woes. The cocky Robin Hood, who'd given the trainer a bit of sass earlier in the day, apparently hadn't spent enough time practicing her new assignment's signature. At one point near the end of our set, a young male guest—just old enough to read, but apparently not old enough to be acquainted with the identities of some of the lesser-known Disney characters appearing in Canada that day—walked back to his mom with a very confused look on his face, as he pondered the page of his just-signed autograph book.

Not knowing any better, he suddenly burst out, loudly enough for all around to hear, "Who's Scroggy Me-Fuck?"

It was hard not to laugh out loud. I did spy the trainer, out of the corner of my eye, give old Mr. Me-Fuck a big thumbs-up after the incident. Needless to say, Uncle Scroggy kept her mouth shut for the rest of training.

The rest of the week saw us go out another three times. Each outing increased in time spent in public. The next day, we did two sets with a short break in between at the Animal Kingdom. I finally got into a new costume: Baloo the Bear from the Disney animated classic *The Jungle Book*. I continued to pace myself and to drink a river of Power-Ade to get myself through, while my body continued to acclimate to the Florida heat, as well as the *Disney* heat inside the costumes. I also kept on with the ibuprofen like it was candy, even though the Baloo costume proved much easier on my neck and joints. First, there wasn't the crazy-heavy head or eye-contact problem to worry about. Second, the girth of the costume—aka Baloo's big belly—provided enough room that there was actually a bit of air circulation inside the costume: no tights or neck fur suffocating my will to live.

We followed that up with a repeat performance in the same location the next day. We did another two sets, but this time I went on as Br'er Bear. While the costume weighed probably five times that of the Goofy costume, the bulk of it was not balanced on top of my head, so it was OK by me. Each time out got a little easier. The real challenge on that second day at the Animal Kingdom was finding enough room in our makeshift dressing room to change, especially considering the monster of a costume I was sporting.

They put the twelve of us up in a very small space that normally served as an office. It had a little desk in one corner, a water cooler in the other—thankfully for me—and that was about it. We had to rotate in and out, three of us changing at a time. Just outside the room was a concrete, pavilion-style structure—no walls—that housed an assortment of metal pens and cages. They were all empty, which made for a slightly eerie scene. That was, until my buddy crawled into one of them to lighten the mood. The trainer was none too happy when he emerged from the room to call in the next three trainees to find Geppetto in full costume growling and pacing like a tiger in the off-limits area.

"*Raaawwwrrr*," said Geppetto, as the trainer approached with a wild look in his eye.

"If someone sees you in there, you'll be terminated," said the livid trainer in a hushed shouting.

"*Meow*."

Those of us witnessing the scene dared not laugh until the trainer once again disappeared into the room.

"This costume's good for rule-breaking. Nobody can get *that* mad at a helpless old man."

"I wouldn't push your luck," I said, still chuckling over the comical confrontation.

"I'll do what I want; I'm not their puppet," he said, grinning. "Eh? See what I did there?"

I shook my head over the bad joke and drained what was left of my water bottle.

The rest of the day went smoothly, as we set up shop in a lightly traveled location that had previously hosted the Pocahontas and Her Forest Friends stage show in the old Camp Minnie-Mickey area of the park. Like Epcot, the Animal Kingdom didn't get the amount of traffic that the Magic Kingdom got, especially during certain times of the day, so it made for a good training ground. Don't get me wrong: *a lot* of guests clamored around once they realized a dozen characters had just shown up, but not the type of people-get-trampled-and-die sort of mob that such a scene could easily inspire in the Magic Kingdom. The relatively *normal* amount of attention shown us at the lesser-attended parks (now, we're talking *Disney* normal, which is arguably not normal at all) allowed us to ease into our new roles and give us a little extra time, as Geppetto might say, to earn our stripes.

We capped off our in-park appearances for the week back at Epcot, where I dog-suited up one last time in World Showcase to conclude my training. My body was finally beginning to regulate temperature a little better inside the costume. The vertebrae in my neck had become permanently fixed in a downward position. My bladder had stretched to hold three Power-Ades' worth of liquid at a time. And my autographs matched the official Goofy signature on my study sheet to a tee—underline and all.

Speaking of, after we were through with our sets for the day, we changed, toweled off, and readied for the final exam we'd been promised at the beginning of the week.

Our trainer took us back outside and we made camp in a breezy backstage "break" location. We spread out on the ground and at the two or three picnic tables set up for lunching cast members.

"This is it: final step before you graduate," said the trainer, as he made his way around the group with papers in hand. Each sheet was divided into four black boxes, completely blank on the inside. He told us to print the name of a single character in our height range at the top of each box and then proceed to sign as close to their official autograph as we could. Once we were finished, we were to bring it to him for his final assessment.

I received two sheets, seeing as how I was required to master eight signatures in my height range before being officially approved to play the roles.

I passed with flying colors, as did the rest of the training group—even Me-Fuck.

Thinking about it afterward, I found it comical how anxious I'd been early in the week over getting my autographs down and passing the big scary exam. Following the eye-opening experience of actually donning full costume and making park appearances, the "signature" challenge just didn't hold the same weight. Between the heat exhaustion, permanent neck problems, and daily migraines, crossing my backwards *F*s in the right place suddenly seemed the least of my worries. Nonetheless, I was relieved to have the test behind me, mostly because it meant training week was all but over.

After the announcement was made that we'd all succeeded in earning the official go-ahead for our specific cast of characters, we hooted and hollered and applauded.

"Thank god," said Scroggy.

"You're welcome," said the trainer smugly.

My buddy and I looked at one another and rolled our eyes.

"Gonna miss this," he said sarcastically.

"Careful!" I scolded in a mock-voice of our fearsome leader, low enough for only the two of us to hear.

We finished the day by participating in brief one-on-one consultations with the trainer, where he sat us each down at a company computer and went over our first week's schedule, where we'd be reporting, and other such details. He also discussed with us the implications of our current color-coding, what it meant exactly, and how we could improve our rankings if we wished. The department held an on-site color-code audition once a month, during which time you could try to boost your scores and elevate your color standing to qualify for different and more movement-intensive characters or roles.

Redemption, I thought to myself, recalling my highly questionable dance routine weeks earlier. But the more I played back the scarring experience in my head, and began to consider all the additional humiliation I'd been put through in the past week, I found myself—at least for the time being—content with my current colors.

"Do you want the details for the next audition?"

"I'm good," I told him.

My schedule was all Goofy for the first week, across various locations. I looked at the six- and eight-hour shifts listed and wondered how I'd ever survive. I figured my only option was to take it as it came. After all, a few days earlier, I'd been skeptical about making it through training alone. And yet, there I was: five pounds lighter, sore as hell, and fully equipped to make magic. The adventure was just beginning.

I shook hands with my now ex-trainer and thanked him for his help the past week.

"I'll see ya out there," he said.

"Yes, you will."

Once we were released for the day, the twelve of us walked—carefully studying our printed schedules as we went—to the backstage bus stop for a ride to the main cast member lot. Tired as we were after a long week of training, we had a seat right there on the sidewalk to wait for our ride. We formed a little circle and began exchanging phone numbers so we could stay in contact now that we were being sent out into the "World." Between the four parks and other sixty-some-thousand cast members, chances were good that we wouldn't be running into one another that often.

Over the course of my Disney career, I kept loose tabs on most of the training group. Besides my buddy, the other male in the group, I saw the other ten infrequently—usually just a passing hello in Costuming in the morning. Only once did I ever work again with one of my training partners: a Goofy and Pluto set at the Animal Kingdom. My buddy and I pushed hard for the scheduling office to pair us together on a Buzz and Woody shift, but alas, it never happened. Apparently, making dreams come true is more of a *guest* thing, rather than a cast-member one.

Still, our friendship continued, and we went on to enjoy many face-offs in Buzz Lightyear's Space Ranger Spin, a ridiculous number of Country Bear Jamborees on days off to pay tribute to our favorite manic-depressive bear, and frequent strolls around World Showcase in an attempt to find him a girlfriend in the International Exchange Program. We also visited one another on set quite often. No matter how much you're around the costumes, the childlike thrill of playing "dress up" never really fades. Hanging out with your buddy and snapping a few pics when he's in full space-ranger getup, sharing secret hand signals with Eeyore at the Crystal Palace breakfast table, or knowingly saluting a Green Army Man as he marches around Pixar Place just doesn't get old.

Unfortunately, not every member of our training group got to experience the magic to the extent that the both of us did.

According to social media, mouthy Me-Fuck got sent home the week after training for getting into it with one of her managers at a set location. The news didn't really shock me. She'd been a firecracker throughout training. It must have been the hot sauce. This girl literally kept a bottle of the stuff in her backpack. Each day, when we'd break for lunch, she'd head to the cast cafeteria and order whatever—pizza, chicken nuggets, fries, a cheeseburger—then just douse it. I sometimes think of her—more her disgusting habit—when I sit down at a restaurant and see a bottle of her brand on the table.

Our group's resident Pluto left a week after that, but by her own choice. Her boyfriend had apparently come down and surprised her from up north to celebrate her finishing training and starting up the new job. While visiting, he popped the question and a diamond ring at the conclusion of Wishes. Pluto left collar and leash behind and happily followed him home.

Wannabee Dora the Explorer lasted about four months before a marriage proposal of her own ended her world travels.

Donald, who'd been studying to be an accountant before taking the job, ended up dropping about thirty pounds after a handful of months in the duck suit. She and her new-and-improved body moved back home and switched her major to Exercise Science.

Max stuck around about just as long, then left to pursue an actual career in the theater—as in roles that allow you to speak and for which drinking gallons of Power-Ade isn't a prerequisite for staying conscious.

One of the skinnier Country Bears actually got pulled by managers almost immediately after training to be a "face character"—the coveted role that's seen as the pinnacle of the Disney-character hierarchy. No fur *and* you can talk. Talk about your transformation: going from Liver Lips McGrowl to Cinderella in a week's time.

Bibbidi-bobbidi-boo! She lasted a couple years, then met her prince, moved away, and lived happily ever after.

Minnie—after a few years in polka dots—moved home and became a man. Like, all-out...surgery and everything. He posted pictures throughout the whole process. Guess Cindy's got nothing on that.

His counterpart, Mickey, had to have knee surgery after a few years on the job, and called it quits. Shortly after, she deleted her Facebook account and none of us ever saw or heard from her again.

Daisy stuck around the company, but transferred out of Entertainment, hoping to find a position she could build a career on. Last I heard, she was working a grill at Pecos Bill's.

The twelfth member of our group outlasted us all and still works in Entertainment, as far as I know. Most likely a lifer. From her humble beginnings as Shaker, the third of our training group's Country Bears, she worked her way up the color ladder to be a mainstay in some of the biggest parades and shows on property. Apparently, her latest gig is playing Mrs. Potts at Hollywood Studio's Beauty and the Beast—Live on Stage. Whenever I catch the show, I imagine my old training-group partner inside that giant teacup and beam with pride.

And, of course, who could forget our lead trainer. We did have a few others that helped out and led various sessions throughout the week, but only one that was with us every step of the way. About six months after training, I ran into one of those assistant trainers in the Mouseketeria in the Magic Kingdom Utilidors and chatted with her over lunch. I got around to asking if she'd run into our lead trainer lately. She said she hadn't, but heard that he left Entertainment and was now somehow involved with Animal Programs over at DAK.

I hoped to god that meant he was scooping up elephant shit.

CHAPTER THREE

The Goof

My first week of shifts took place at Epcot, which made me feel a little more comfortable about being all alone: at least the scenery would be familiar. But even that small amount of comfort didn't end up panning out, as I checked in at Character Base—a building adjacent to Costuming—after a weekend of much-needed rest.

"You'll be going to C-Spot," said the man in charge.

I nodded, pretending to know what that meant.

He sensed my uncertainty and clarified. "Character Spot...in Future World."

"Oh, right," I said, "I've been there."

"Great! Have a good day."

"As a guest, I mean," I explained.

"Gotcha," he said, showing sympathy and taking some time to help me get my bearings. "Head over to Costuming and pack your bag. Van picks you up in..." He glanced at the clock on the wall to the left of his desk. "Forty-five."

I thanked him for his help and made my way to Costuming.

I picked up a big black bag off the rack and began down the aisles, filling it up as I went, as if I was on a shopping spree—though, in actuality, I'd never be able to afford anything off those shelves. We'd had a whole informational session during training about Costuming—how the operation worked, the various roles performed in the department, how the costumes were designed, made, repaired, and, of course, how much they cost. Really, I think they were just trying to scare us into taking good care of everything we wore. Still, I didn't want to misplace a shoe, or put a dent in a mask, and forfeit a couple months' pay to cover the cost.

"I guarantee none of you has ever owned a pair of shoes this expensive," the trainer had said on our initial walkthrough, carefully picking up a pair of Minnie's heels.

Of course, the group loudmouth protested, claiming her closet was full of designer wear that put the custom, hand-painted shoes he was holding to shame. "Nuh-uh," she said with her usual attitude, "not unless those things cost more than two grand."

Embarrassed, he set them down, never revealing their cost. He quickly scanned the room for something more expensive.

It was kind of fun to watch him be put in his place.

After spouting off some very high prices of various costume accessories, which didn't seem to faze our snobbish training partner in the least, he finally pulled out the big guns. "The Mike Wazowski costume costs *fifty* grand to make."

"Sounds like one of those Disney urban legends to me," I whispered to my buddy.

"Lemme guess, she's got a dress that cost that much," he replied.

She didn't, but instead accused the trainer of being a liar.

He finally just gave up. "Break it and see how much they charge you."

Thankfully, Mike wasn't an Epcot resident, so I didn't have to worry about any bankruptcy-inducing mishaps while browsing the aisles—say, tripping over one of his monster feet and cracking an eyeball.

The first items into my bag were six pairs of basics: one for each of my scheduled sets for the day. Next, I moved to the tights section and threw in a pair of both the leg and arm variety. Costuming was kind enough to assemble the main pieces of every costume on a hanger, so cast members didn't have to roam the aisles looking for the individual pieces. I grabbed a hanger laden with the traditional Goofy outfit that I'd become well-acquainted with during training: pants, shirt, and neck fur. On the rack above was a bin of suspenders, from which I grabbed a pair. I spotted the shoe section and headed over, careful not to bump any of the several-hundred-dollar heels on my way over to the faux-leather cheapies that I'd be sweating in all day. I grabbed a left and a right of the one-size-fits-none footwear and made my way over to the heads. I loved walking up and down the rows of masks—all those iconic faces smiling as I passed. I found the Goofys and started checking the stickers on the back of the heads on each of the ten or so masks there.

Costuming used the stickers—each marked with a day of the week—to let cast members know if a particular head was ready for use. Once a used head was returned after a shift, someone from Costuming would sanitize it by spraying an aerosol can of poisonous chemicals inside and throwing a sticker on the outside to mark the death date of all accumulated bacteria. The head was then re-shelved, but avoided until at least two to three days had passed and the harmful cleaning solution had aired out, for the most part. Cast members, when selecting their heads, knew to look only for those with stickers that predated the current day by a sufficient amount of time. It was Monday, so I found myself a Wednesday, just to be on the extra-safe side, and then made a quick stop at the headgear bin.

Amid the tangles, I managed to pull one out that was still in relatively good shape. The majority of plastic pieces were held together by duct-tape. *$50,000 costumes, my ass*. I grabbed a handful of skull caps and a few fresh towels for the day and stuffed them into my bag, which was now about as heavy as I was. I turned and surveyed the room, going through a mental checklist to make sure I hadn't forgotten anything. Satisfied, I approached the checkout lanes and hoisted my haul up on the counter. Cast members with handheld scanners would go through and scan every single item and piece of clothing in your possession. Those barcodes weren't just for basics.

The woman working was pleasant, and chatted as she scanned. After she'd finished, she looked thoughtfully at the bag for a moment, then said, "Gloves. You're missing gloves."

"Right!" I said, jogging over to the glove bin to retrieve a pair.

"Get two sets."

I looked at her curiously.

"Character Glove," she stated matter-of-factly.

I nodded knowingly and took her advice.

Once the rather lengthy process of assembling and checking-out my costume was through, I headed for the common area to do a bit of prepping before my van pick-up. Stepping over dozens of black bags—Costuming was a buzz of character performers in the morning—I took a seat on a long wooden bench and started sizing my headgear. When I was satisfied with the fit, I headed to the restroom and slipped into a pair of basics. On my way back, I stopped for a good two minutes at the drinking fountain, not wanting to fall behind on my hydration routine on my first full-length day in the parks. I settled back onto the bench and started buttoning the yellow suspenders to Goofy's blue trousers, in order to save a little time once I arrived at the set location.

The girl next to me had just pulled her hair back into a ponytail and was slipping a sweat band over her head. I noticed a yellow high heel peeking out of her bag, marking her as Minnie.

"Hey, did you know those things cost..."

"Yeah," she said, cutting me off and rolling her eyes. She followed it up with a smile, however, and introduced herself. "C-Spot?" she asked, eyeing the pair of suspender-ed pants in my lap.

I nodded.

"Have we worked together before?" she said, studying my face.

"I don't think so."

Minnie squinted as if thinking hard about where she might know me from. "You sure?"

"It's my first day," I finally admitted.

"Oh, shit. No way!"

"Yep."

"You're gonna hate it."

My eyes grew wide.

"Yeah, C-Spot's the worst."

"Really?"

"Nah, it's fine. You coming to warm-ups?"

"Uhh...yeah." In my haste to put my costume together and not miss my pick-up, I'd forgotten about the requisite pre-shift calisthenics for every character performer. A few days removed from training, and already I was losing it.

"Let's go. Van will be here in fifteen."

We started down the hall. I let her take the lead. Though I'd visited the workout room once during training, I didn't trust myself to find it again. We made a couple turns and finally landed in a room full of weights and mats. A smattering of basics-wearing individuals were stretching and chatting. An older gentleman, who looked to be in better shape than anyone in the room, was queuing up a boom box at the front of the room. He said hello and reminded us to sign in. I added my name to the clipboard just as the music began.

"Morning, everybody," he said. "It's gonna be a great day."

We all formed loose lines and followed along through a brief set of warm-ups.

After we finished, I headed to the water cooler in the corner of the room and drank four cones' worth of ice-cold water.

"Van should be here," said Minnie.

I gulped one more down as fast as I could and followed her back to the common area.

I slung my black bag over my shoulder and took it out to the fifteen-passenger that had just pulled up to the door.

The driver took the bag from me and toted it around to the rear of the vehicle. "Hop in," he told me.

Four others, Minnie included, piled in after me.

The ride over, via the backstage roads, was pretty quiet, other than the talk radio that the driver was listening to.

I looked out the window and tried to pump myself up for the shift ahead. *Six sets. I can do this.*

When the van stopped and we retrieved our bags, I again fell to the back since I hadn't the slightest idea where I was going.

"Come on, newbie," Minnie called.

Arriving at our destination, my new friend was kind enough to give me the rundown. "Set schedule's posted here," she said, pointing to the wall. "Goofy's area is over there. Your switch-out should be here in a few minutes."

I'd forgotten that unlike training I'd no longer be the only Goof in town. Each location facilitated two of each character, so that both could essentially take turns being onstage. I looked at the schedule on the wall. "Forty-minute sets?" I said out loud.

"Yeah, indoor sets are a little longer," said Minnie. "Since they're air conditioned."

I opened my mouth to complain, but was interrupted by a manager who'd just walked in. "Let's get a move on. Park's gonna be busy today."

The five of us set about getting into costume.

The other Goofy entered just in time to help me with my neck fur. He was already drinking a Power-Ade. *Smart man.*

Five character attendants strode in, and the volume of the room escalated. Between discussions about their love lives—or rather their complaints about the lack there-of—they spot-checked and readied us for show time.

"Goof, this suspender's on backwards," said my attendant, sighing heavily as she fixed the problem. "All set."

"Who's on rope-drop?" said the manager, with a sense of urgency in her voice.

"Not it," said Mickey.

"I did it yesterday," said Donald.

"Me and Goof," said Minnie, volunteering and putting her arm in mine.

"Rope drop? What's that mean?"

"It's fun."

Pluto laughed from the corner.

"Well, it's easy," she said, as we, along with our two attendants, headed out to the set location, through the double doors, and into the park.

Ahead, I saw a crowd of guests go crazy at the sight of us. They were, however, contained by a rope strung from two portable stanchions guarded by a couple of cast members with headsets on.

As we neared, cameras began flashing and people began shouting our names, as if we were true celebrities.

Even though I still had no clue what I was doing out there, I couldn't help but grin inside the mask.

"One minute 'til opening," announced one of the cast members excitedly.

The crowd cheered.

Minnie let go of my arm and headed straight for them. She knelt down in front of a timid little girl and gave her an exaggerated smooch on the cheek.

I walked up and patted the girl on the head.

Minnie started pointing to the crowd and subtly shooing me away.

I got the hint and went and found a child of my own to dote on.

The cast member with the headset began a countdown from ten, and the whole crowd joined in.

Minnie grabbed her child's hand, so I did the same.

The rope fell to the ground and Minnie and her new best friend led the charge into the park, hand-in-hand.

I followed close behind, toting along an excited preteen boy who couldn't stop blabbering about how he was dying to ride Test Track.

We led the guests and their families all the way back to C-Spot, where I claimed a section of the large room as my own and began interacting with guests.

"Silly Goof," said my attendant loudly, "that's Donald's area."

The crowd chuckled, as I played off the mistake by looking around frantically like I was lost, throwing my arms up in the air in desperation, then burying my face in my gloves out of embarrassment.

Just then, the Duck himself emerged and pretended to kick my rear-end back to my designated meet-and-greet area.

The guests in line roared.

My attendant led me to the correct spot. "Stay," she said, a bit firmer than I thought was necessary.

Flustered and already out of breath, I began receiving the line of enthusiastic guests. *So much for pacing myself.*

I eventually calmed down and got into a rhythm. The air conditioning did make a difference; I was thankful for that. When my attendant announced that the next family would be my last before I had to "go check on Max," I felt a tinge of excitement in my chest. *Made it! One down, five to go.*

Things were not as hunky-dory back in the dressing room, however. The second the five of us re-entered the backstage area, the manager let us have it. On a whiteboard, she'd scrawled estimates of how many guests we'd seen during our set, and how many we *should have seen*, in order to keep pace with the line and the park's expected attendance for the day. "Way behind," she scolded.

"It's not me," said Mickey.

The rest chimed in with similar sentiments.

Minnie looked over at me and chuckled. "Newbie!" she said, pointing an accusatory finger.

The manager looked me up and down. "New recruit?"

"Yep."

"Love and shove, Goof. Love and shove," she said, then exited the room in a huff.

I sighed and walked over to drown my cares in a Power-Ade. After a few gulps, I stripped down to my soaking-wet basics and ducked behind the makeshift curtain in the corner of the room to put on a dry pair. I took a seat on the floor next to my black bag and finished my drink. I sat for the next fifteen minutes or so in silence, giving myself a pep talk about picking up the pace. Still a relatively slow dresser, compared to the veteran character performers, I rose and began changing while my fellow characters continued to read their books or play on their phones. When set-time came, I pulled my gloves tight and headed back out, determined to show the rest of them that I could keep up. I returned afterward with that old familiar feeling from training week: exhaustion.

"Better," said the manager, posting more figures on the whiteboard. "But keep pushing."

The rest of the day was a race—against myself, to improve productivity, and against the clock, to meet the manager's demands. I steadily got faster with each set. After coming in for the final time, our team was rewarded with a big, grateful "That'll have to do," before being told to pack up and head outside to the van.

All in all, not the most magical experience.

I ended up working C-Spot shifts pretty frequently throughout my time in Entertainment. It was always one of my least favorite spots to work. The nature of the location and the amount of traffic it received just made for a relatively chaotic experience most times.

Also detracting from the magic at C-Spot was a particularly bothersome Donald who worked there. A few times a year, the department would allow full-time cast members to "bid" for specific set locations, and the assignments would be doled out based on seniority, the number of bids received, and other factors. Specifically, the mice and ducks who were regulars—meaning they'd been granted their bids and were scheduled there full time—weren't the most pleasant people in the world. They were rude, had chips on their shoulders, and seemed to hate their jobs—and guests, for that matter. Donald was by far the worst.

Compounding the problem—and I want to say this in the nicest way possible—was her frighteningly bad looks. Now, I'm not exaggerating when I tell you that this brand of ugly wasn't your average, everyday, majority-of-the-human-population ugly, but horror-movie level—buck teeth, missing teeth, the smallest beady eyes you've ever seen, pig nose, stringy unwashed hair—kind of like the real-life version of Madam Mim from *The Sword in the Stone*.

The shudder-worthy sight was heightened by her being so damn tiny; her freakishly small size pushed the creepiness-factor right off the charts.

Anytime I worked there, I just couldn't help but think of how disturbed parents would be if they knew *what* was wrapping its arms around their precious little children. And I certainly couldn't imagine what kinds of reactions would be elicited if the kids themselves could have seen what was under the costume.

Of course, it didn't help matters that her two buck teeth were pretty much the only ones left in her mouth, her hair looked and smelled as if it hadn't been washed since the park's opening, and one of her beady little eyes would start twitching uncontrollably if you looked her in the face any longer than a glance. Anytime I worked there, I couldn't help but wonder what all those happy parents clicking away on their cameras would think if they could glimpse the real Donald, if only for a moment. I certainly knew how the kids themselves would have reacted. Hell, to this day, I do my best to refrain from Donald meet-and-greets—any Donald, any park. I've just never been able to look at the costume the same. No matter where I am, whenever I get too close, all I do is imagine that face on the other side of the mouth screen. Who knows where she bid next? She could be anywhere. All I'm saying is hug at your own risk.

My next scheduled set location within the Experimental Prototype Community of Tomorrow was an out-of-the-way spot in Innoventions West, known affectionately by character performers as Visa.

While C-Spot took the cake for my least favorite location in the park, Visa was one of the best: small, not very crowded, and slow-paced enough to make some serious magic. If you didn't get the memo, or you're an American-Express kinda person, Visa is cast-member slang for the private meet-and-greet location reserved exclusively for Disney Visa cardholders. Guests who show their card are able to stop by and play with a couple of characters and even snag a complimentary photo. Disney likes to advertise the location by saying that guests can look forward to an assortment of random, "surprise" characters with each new visit. In actuality, there are only ever three:

Minnie, Goofy, and Pluto. And I was one of them, countless times during my tenure as the Goof.

When I worked there, we were on a rotating schedule, so only two of us went out at a time: either Minnie and Goofy or Minnie and Pluto.

Guests were infrequent. Sometimes, we'd go a whole half-hour set and only see a few. The PhotoPass photographer and character attendant were usually casual and lax on the rules because of the low amount of traffic, so as long as no guests were around, we chatted and played games onstage in our costumes. No "love and shove" there. When a family did stop by, we were able to go through a full and complete interaction with them—spend time with each family member, sign autographs, pose for pictures, maybe play a game of tag or hide-and-seek using the room's curtain and wooden, cartoon-style backdrop.

Backstage was also somewhat of a free-for-all. The three characters working a given shift all shared a dressing room that amounted to little more than a closet. It was rectangular, and barely able to hold three black bags and their owners. If a character attendant wanted in, either the bags had to be stacked or somebody had to step out of the room. Nine times out of ten, I was stuffed into said closet with two girls—Minnie and Pluto were almost always played by females—and made to change alongside them. Seeing as how nearly every girl in Entertainment was straight, and almost every guy in Entertainment wasn't, the mood could easily turn awkward (and painfully desperate) when they realized I was an exception.

"You can just change in here; you don't have to go to the bathroom," was usually the pat response from either Minnie or Pluto or both upon returning from set, and seeing me pull out a fresh set of basics from my bag.

I'd just nod and leave anyway.

After the next set, they'd coax further. "I've been in theater my whole life; I'm used to it," Minnie would say, unzipping her polka-dot dress and letting it fall to the floor. "Guys and girls are naked all the time in theater; no one cares," Pluto would add, as she shed her fur.

I'd continue to ignore them. Usually, the comments died down a few sets in, once they saw that I wasn't going to budge. Still, I couldn't control their side of things, so when all was said and done, I ended up seeing a hell of a lot more sports bras and undies during my Visa career than I did guests.

One advantage of being a newbie with no bid-location home was that my role status was considered "global," meaning that I could be scheduled freely throughout any of the parks, hotels, or restaurants on property. After Epcot, my next schedule took me into the deepest, darkest jungles of Disney's Animal Kingdom. DAK (rhymes with yak), as it was known by cast members, had a different vibe than all the other parks—at least, backstage. The nature of the landscaping and animal habitats incorporated throughout both the onstage and backstage areas accounted for much of the difference. They didn't have the extensive access roads found in the backstage areas of other parks, and the place overall was a lot larger, more expansive. So much so that the cast member bus stop and parking area were still a good half-mile (or more) from the nearest backstage facilities—Costuming, in particular.

So, Disney provided nearly a hundred bikes, known as DAK-cycles, for cast member use. There was a massive bike rack, filled to capacity, at the cast bus stop, and another matching one just outside the entrance to the main backstage structure, which contained the costuming department. I always enjoyed shifts at DAK, if only for the built-in bike ride that came with it. Something about a morning ride through the backstage of the

Animal Kingdom—monkeys howling, birds singing in the distance—put me in an extra-good mood to start the day. And, after a long, hot shift, the wind in my hair complemented a relaxing cooldown before boarding the bus back to reality.

Once inside Costuming, the process looked and worked very much the same as it did in Epcot. Though, for my first shift there, I had a little more on my black-bag shopping list than I was accustomed to. I was scheduled for meet-and-greets in the now-defunct Camp Minnie-Mickey section of the park, and Goofy, along with the other characters, had a customized outfit for the area.

One thing I really enjoyed doing, whenever I had a little extra time in the mornings, was browsing Goof's wide-ranging wardrobe on the racks. A manager once told me that everyone's favorite dog (sorry, Pluto) had somewhere in the neighborhood of seventy-five different costume iterations. I'm sure there are probably even more now.

The variations for the Camp Minnie-Mickey shift alone were numerous. In fact, the only things that stayed the same were the shoes and gloves. Everything else was a different color or style altogether. The hobo pants were traded in for green khakis (remember, it's a camping theme). The shirt turned yellow plaid and was complemented by a cargo-style vest with mesh pockets, a few sewn-on scouting patches, and matching brown-khaki socks. I even got a small plastic compass to keep in one of my pockets to pull out during guest-interactions if I wanted—a fun idea, but once it went into the pocket before a set, I never remembered it was there. Plus, do you know how hard it was to reach into a tiny vest pocket with gloved hands the likes of the Stay Puft Marshmallow Man? I was also issued a neckerchief, which was nice because I didn't have to worry as much about my neck fur being perfect. Finally, the whole thing was capped off with...well, a cap. Not the incredibly heavy, stovepipe variety, but a nice, sensible, *cloth* baseball-style cap.

Of course, it took me quite a bit longer in Costuming to round up all the extras. The damn compass, especially, was impossible to find. I finally had to call on one of the wardrobe scanners up front for help. It turned out they were tucked away in a wire bin on top of a clothes rack, almost out of reach, next to a bunch of tiaras. I found it slightly ironic that the only piece of wardrobe I hadn't been able to find was a *compass*, and the cast member and I had a good laugh over it.

Once I was packed, I checked out and headed over to warm-ups. The man in charge was gruff and burly, and sported a Chicago Cubs hat and t-shirt. As he queued up the music, he talked in a booming voice of the company softball league, warning some cast-member friends that they didn't stand a chance in an upcoming game. He was the first straight guy I'd seen in weeks; his machismo seemed oddly out-of-place in a room full of dainty Tinker Bells and bouncy Tiggers. The boom box behind him began playing a Cyndi Lauper tune and a big, non-threatening smile washed over his face.

"Good choice," one of his softball buddies called out.

"Jack and I listen to this every morning; it's our alarm," he said, suddenly turning into the biggest gay in the room. *All was right again in the Disney World.*

Following warm-ups, I was golf-carted over to the set location, since it was too close to justify a van-ride, but too far to hoof it. Less than an hour at work and I'd already ridden a bus, bike, and golf cart—not to mention jogged a half-mile in place to "Girls Just Want to Have Fun." If nothing else, Disney kept things interesting.

The dressing room was a wide-open, circular area with maybe a dozen or more curtained "stalls" along the outside wall, where individuals could change into costume. The room was absolutely abuzz with chatter and confusion, as mice, ducks, bunnies, and munks (character slang for Chip and Dale) scrambled around the room, half-human, half-animal.

Two attendants greeted me at the door. "Goof?" one of them asked.

"Yep."

"You'll need these," she said, pulling out a handful of very sharp pins from a plastic container and placing them in my palm.

I gave her a concerned look.

"For your hat—gotta pin it on."

"Ah." I headed for a vacant stall and began prepping my costume.

I worked for ten minutes trying to fix the cap onto Goofy's head. The pins just wouldn't cooperate, considering the head itself was made of a hard, sturdy plastic material. Finally, after pricking my fingers a few dozen times and dropping half my stash on the floor, I set out for help.

Three steps towards the attendants at the door, and I stopped dead in my tracks. "Yeeeooowww!" I winced in pain, and hopping on one foot, pulled a pin out of the bottom of my other.

"That's why shoes are required," scolded one of the attendants, who was walking over. She pointed at the giant sign on the wall: SHOES MUST BE WORN AT ALL TIMES.

I grinned sheepishly.

"Give me that," she said, taking Goofy's head and pinning down the cap in less than thirty seconds.

"How did you..."

"The pin goes into this thin layer of fur, just above the plastic."

I took back the head curiously and studied her work.

"Get that thing on—you're up."

I tip-toed my way back to my bag, trying to avoid any more stray tetanus, and finished dressing as quickly as

I could. A minute later, I raced over to the exit door and lined up with the other outgoing characters. Tired and out of breath. *I couldn't keep starting my sets like this.*

Goofy's set location for Camp Minnie-Mickey was under a shaded log structure, in keeping with the theme, and I had to walk a somewhat lengthy winding trail through the woods—also apparently keeping with the theme—to get there. It wasn't a bad gig. The much-lighter mask was a nice change of pace. But, in all honesty, the weight differential threw me and screwed up my neck position and eye-contact levels, since I was accustomed to the heavier load. Plus, I was paired with Donald. Over the course of my Camp shifts, never *ugly* Donald, thank god, but a fair share of annoying ones.

Character pairings were hit-and-miss. In my experience, mostly miss. Every now and then, my partner was cool, chill, and easy to get along with, so we'd have a blast performing together on set. But usually not. Some were indifferent toward me or to guests; others were stiff and anal about the rules and would perform like robots. On occasion, I'd get one who wouldn't stop talking before and after sets.

My Donald on that first DAK shift was too ornery for her own good. She'd sign an autograph and then slam the book closed and un-click the pen before handing it to me, thinking it funny to watch me try to perform the impossible task of flipping to the appropriate page with character gloves on. In pictures, she'd "jokingly" pose right in front of me to block me out of the shot. The PhotoPass photographer, who for some reason insisted on encouraging her, would play along for the guests and fake-scold her: "Now, Donald, we know you're a rock star, but you can't be the focus of *every* shot."

The family would giggle and Donald would pretend to be angry and stomp off and take his place alongside me, at which time I'd start to feel pinches up and down my back—Donald again, teasing me and trying to get me to break my pose.

After a couple sets in, I'd gotten wise to the duck's antics and started placing enough family members between us during photos that she could no longer reach me. I also became very quick at grabbing the book and pen from her hands, just as she was finishing the last letter of her signature, so she didn't have time to close it. Needless to say, I took great pleasure in the mishap I discovered halfway through the day, when I ripped the book out of her hands and readied to place my own signature beside...*Daisy's*? She'd signed the wrong name, which wasn't actually that uncommon, seeing as how many character performers switched roles on a daily basis, sometimes playing multiple roles in a single day. But I couldn't have been happier to see it happen to my cocky little shit of a partner in that moment. I Goofy-laughed (hand over mouth screen, head and body bobbing and shaking joyously) my head off.

She stood there, not knowing what to make of my actions.

I shoved the page up against her beak-screen, and once she saw her blunder, she grabbed for the book.

But I was too quick. I snatched it away, signed my name, and closed it emphatically. I handed it back to the teenage-girl owner and quickly positioned her on the opposite side of where Donald stood, so there was no chance of my co-worker getting at the book again.

I dropped to a kneeling pose for the picture, so as not to get any back pinches, and just as the camera began to click, subtly reached my hand back and around to the calves of the duck tights and pinched as hard and as many times as my gloves would allow.

Donald dared not bring up the incident in the dressing room following the set, since she was the one who'd been at fault for signing the wrong name. Managers didn't look kindly on that sort of thing. I didn't have any more problems with her for the rest of the day, or ever again, when we happened to be scheduled together. And I had quite a few camp days during my time with the company. Even still, never once did I break out that damn compass.

Another set location that I frequented at the park was DinoLand U.S.A. Neon green shorts, another vest and neckerchief, checkered shirt, and an even lighter hat, which I finally got the hang of pinning to my head. I ought to have, since my first shift there was around eleven hours in length. I couldn't even believe what I was seeing when the schedule first came out. I figured it was some sort of mistake. But, arriving at the park via my DAK-cycle that morning and asking around a bit, I came to find out EMH (that's Extra Magic Hours) shifts were quite common.

I was nervous; I didn't even know if my body could handle such a thing. On the way out to the set location, I made the van driver stop at the cast cafeteria, and I literally came out with a sack full of groceries. I knew my body needed a little something extra—or a lot—to survive the record number of hours and sets.

Thankfully, I was paired with a Pluto from training, who was as nervous as I was about the prospect of dying a slow, painful death in Dino-wasteland to the shouts of midway carnival barkers, Primeval Whirl-induced screaming, and the ridiculously bad—yet hell of a catchy—tune of Chester and Hester's theme song. Talking about it out loud helped to lessen the anxiety, as well as being able to pass along our final wishes through each other (the *if-I-don't-make-it-tell-my-mom-I-love-her* sort of thing), just in case.

Another bit of saving grace came in the form of her Pluto double, with whom she alternated sets. He was one of only a few male Plutos that I worked with and something of a Martha Stewart wannabe. Upon arriving for our extra-long stay in DinoLand, he informed us that

there was a home-made casserole in the fridge and a picnic basket of plates and silverware for our use that he'd
brought along from home. It couldn't have been better
timing, as the four helpings of cheesy, delicious carbs,
paired with my own haul of fruit, fruit-flavored breakfast
pastries, chicken-salad sandwich, turkey sandwich, two
bags of Sun Chips, and lake of Power-Ade were enough to
sustain me to park closing—which ended up being memorable on its own account.

As we neared the end of our final set in front of
our wooden backdrop, fashioned to look like a giant
DinoLand postcard, our character attendant closed the
line—meaning, though we were still meeting guests, no
new ones were allowed to queue up. Tired as we were, the
realization that we'd nearly survived our hellish day gave
us all an energy boost—attendant included.

This particular attendant was a young guy, about my
age, who was fun-loving and laid-back. The two of us
got along really well, and I ended up working with him
countless times. Though he was a little short and sported
a so-so haircut, he very much fancied himself a ladies'
man. He often could be found, throughout the course of
a set, neglecting his duties in favor of chatting up a few
girls in line. That said, he was still good at his job, and
always serious when he needed to be.

The three of us, counting Pluto, had started to get
slap-happy, and after we bid goodbye to our final guest
of the night, started horsing around onstage: giving each
other high fives, locking arms and *dosey doe-ing* in circles
around our postcard set.

"Your fly's down again, Goof," said the attendant.

I fell for it and looked, then gave him a nice, big Goofy-
laugh—though the joke stung a bit more than it should
have, seeing as how I had come onset earlier in the day
with the fly of my neon-green Dino-shorts wide open,
tucked-in red-checkered shirt sticking out the hole.

Thankfully, my attendant-friend had caught the snafu relatively early—maybe only five or six families in—and taken me around behind the backdrop to zip me up.

"Smooth one," he said, as he remedied the wardrobe malfunction.

If my neck hadn't been pressed down into my chest as far as it would go, I would have hung my head in shame.

When he brought it up again at the end of the night, I was a good sport about it. I figured I owed him one; he could have, after all, chosen not to say anything and let me appear in hundreds of vacation photos with what, from a distance, looked like a tiny red-and-white checked penis flopping out of my already hideous-looking shorts.

As we were laughing over my gullibility—him out loud, Pluto and I silently—a weary-looking mom approached and shoved her two children forward. "Let's get a picture and get outta here," she said, unamused.

The children darted up to the beginning of the line, which was closed off with a chain. They ducked under and started making their way to us.

Our attendant approached the woman—probably twenty years his senior—and apologized, telling her the line was closed and the characters were just leaving.

She swore and told him she didn't understand why he couldn't just make an exception. "They're standing right there, for chrissakes," she said.

"I'm sorry, ma'am, I really am." He lowered his voice a bit. "Company policy—it's for the performers' safety."

"What about your safety?" she snapped back and acted as if she might belt him across the face.

He only chuckled at the threat and turned to walk away.

"I'll tell you what..." she said flabbergasted, but then trailed off. She eyed her kids. "Give mom a sec," she told them, as she grabbed the attendant's hand and led him back around the postcard and out of sight.

Considering my close proximity, I was still able to hear some of their conversation.

"Look, what do you want?" she said. "I'll give it to you right now. Hand? Mouth? What's it gonna take?"

I heard the attendant laugh nervously, then mumble something I couldn't make out.

Her voice lowered as well, and there was sporadic conversation for the next minute or so.

I'm not exactly sure what was said between the two of them, or what—if anything—went on back there, but once the pair reappeared, the woman left in a huff with her kids in tow. "Let's get outta here," she yelled, the kids crying and complaining as they went.

The attendant walked up next to me and sighed heavily.

"We'll come back tomorrow. You workin'?" she called back, then started cackling, before the three of them disappeared into the night.

"Let's get inside quick," he said, ushering us offstage.

Once safe, the attendant, who believed I'd been oblivious to the situation, looked me straight in the mouth screen and began telling me the story.

"I know," I said, stopping him.

His eyes grew wider, and he appeared slightly concerned.

"Your fly's down," I told him.

He looked immediately, his hands reaching for his crotch, before he caught on to the joke.

I gave him a big Goofy-laugh, this time fully audible.

Another memorable experience came a few days later. Thankfully, I hadn't been scheduled sun-up to sun-down, so I had a little more spring in my size thirty-six step when quite possibly the biggest Goofy fans in the world set foot in DinoLand. They were a pair of twenty-something girls from Japan dressed in homemade Goofy-print dresses and Goofy souvenir hats—not unlike the one I'd gotten as a child—and carried bags full of gifts for their hero...their hero being *me*. They couldn't speak a word of English. Actually, I take that back. They spoke a single word of English, actually more like shouted. And their heavy accents took their toll on the pronunciation. The second the two of them arrived at the front of the line, they started bawling tears of joy. They were literally hyperventilating, as they began repeatedly shouting a version of my name that sounded something like *Go-ewww-fee*. They didn't even see Pluto as they clung to my checkered shirt with a tightness that made me wonder if they'd ever let go. They did, only to retrieve the offerings they'd brought in my honor.

First out of the bags was a collection of origami animals they'd made especially for me. They placed them one-by-one into my padded palms, until there were too many to hold and the character attendant had to come over to help. Next up was a basket of fruit, complete with handwritten love notes tucked between the pieces. Some handcrafted paper necklaces followed, along with several plastic Goofy figurines they had apparently purchased back home. The attendant collected my haul as I thanked them with countless hugs and some extra-loud lip-smack smooches on their cheeks and hands, after which they shed a few tears and jumped up and down in place like hysterical teenage girls in one of those old clips from a Beatles concert. I sure felt like a rock star.

The spectacle was so amusing to those around that the attendant let the girls stay and visit with me for several minutes, and the rest of the line didn't even care. To make light of the fact that he—rather, she—was being ignored, Pluto—alone, off in the corner of the set location—started running around in circles, chasing her tail, to the delight of the crowd. After what amounted to a whole photo shoot's worth of pictures, the girls reluctantly tore themselves away, or were more accurately *pulled* away by the attendant, blowing kisses and crying out, "Go-ewww-fee," as they went. They continued from as far away as Primeval Whirl, and when the set ended ten or fifteen minutes later, they were right there along the path to our exit off-stage to get another touch. I half-expected them to faint when I acquiesced and reached out a character glove to meet their expectant hands. Meanwhile, Pluto moped along behind, next to our character attendant with rolling eyes and arms full of the goodies I'd received. Our switch-outs were waiting on the other side of the fence, and we stopped to tell of the fan girls that awaited.

"Sorry, man," I said to the other Goofy, shrugging and pointing toward my load of gifts.

"What's that?" said a muffled voice.

"Treasures...from the Far East," I said, laughing. I grabbed an origami bird from the attendant's arms and flew it toward his mouth-screen.

He laughed and started to flap his arms like a bird.

The attendant impatiently handed over the many presents she'd been toting.

As I struggled to hold them, I patted my comrade on the back. "Go get 'em."

He headed onstage, and even as I walked toward our modular, I could hear the ecstatic shouting resume in the distance.

Unfortunately, I was demoted from rock star to stagehand in almost no time at all, as later that day I was approached backstage during lunch break by our PhotoPass photographer.

"Hey, I need to talk to you," he said.

Seeing a PhotoPass cast member in our character trailer was odd enough, but the fact that I'd never spoken a word to the man in my life made the confrontation all the more nerve-racking.

"Sure," I said, trying to sound unfazed by the strange request.

"Not here; follow me."

He led me out the door and to another nearby modular. Inside sat a handful of PhotoPass cast members on break. We walked the length of the room, around the corner, and into a small office space that featured a wall of what looked to be television screens. They were actually computer monitors, which I realized as the man logged into the unit on the corner desk and brought up several pictures, all containing some very familiar faces—as in, the guests I'd just met and greeted fifteen minutes earlier on-set.

"Eye-contact's way off," said the man gruffly. "Here, here, and here." He pointed out my mask in three of the pictures.

"Really?" I said, not seeing much of a problem.

He looked at me, eyes narrowing, and seemed angry that I'd questioned him. "It's *bad show*," he said. "Try and get it right next set."

I looked down at the man. Way down. And suddenly realized *that* was the problem. The guy was practically mouse height, which meant that for me to look him—or his camera—in the eye, I'd practically have to be on my knees. "My neck doesn't bend that far," I said, hoping not to insult him, but on the other hand, kind of hoping to.

"Well, you shouldn't be wearing the costume then."

I felt like fighting him, but controlled my annoyance over the man's power-play. "OK, I'll try harder."

"Good, because my manager won't let these fly, and I'm not letting this come back on me," he said.

I turned around and walked back to my modular without another word.

I discussed the matter with Pluto, and she, familiar with the man herself from previous shifts, said simply, "I hate that guy."

During the next set, any time I posed for a photo, in addition to straining my neck as far down as it would go,

I also bent at the waist—almost as if I was reaching down to pick something up off the floor—in order to at least attempt to point my painted-on eyeballs straight at Short Stuff's camera.

Afterward, he poked his head into the modular and said, "Gettin' there."

I was steaming. In the next set—which was also the final one of the day—I blatantly disregarded his orders and made sure my mask was practically staring up at the ceiling for photos. Pluto was in on it, and made sure to look down at the floor for every picture, so that there wasn't a single character eyeball in the shot making contact with the lens.

Pluto and I were Group 1 that day, meaning we were the earlier character group, finishing the last of our sets just as Group 2 went out for the location's last meet-and-greet of the day. So, the puppy and I were back at Costuming, scanning all our items into the system and dumping them in the appropriate laundry bins, while our bossy PhotoPass-friend was busy finishing up his own shift. We did leave him a note on the table of the modular, however, knowing full well he'd stop in after he'd finished to see if either of us troublemakers was still around. Thankfully, I never saw or worked with him again after that, and our "Here's looking at you!" note, signed Goofy and Pluto with two tiny pupils drawn into the Os in *Goofy*, were the last words ever spoken between us.

It wasn't long after the DinoLand drama that I was finally scheduled for the big show: Magic Kingdom, that is. Or, again, simply MK to cast members.

That was one of the hallmarks of backstage Disney, by the way: the lingo, vocabulary, verbiage...whatever you want to call it. Cast members learned and spoke fluently—sometimes created—their very own vernacular when it came to their beloved work environment.

Every attraction, show, restaurant, and location on property got the treatment. Usually, the name was just shortened by a few syllables, but if at all possible, someone, somewhere would try their best to acronym-ize it. Those were the ones cast members were extra-proud to throw around: your DAKs, MKs, or even MI-SI-CIs (pronounced like a fraternity and meant to refer to the former parade/show, Move It, Shake It, Celebrate It). But that didn't mean your Fants (Fantasmic), Thunders (Big Thunder Mountain Railroad), or T-Spins (Triceratop Spin) were any less popular. I always enjoyed the in-park radio code that many cast members were trained on and used, whether over walkie-talkies, headsets, or attraction phone systems—my all-time favorites being Code V and protein spill. Both were interchangeable and used to politely report an upchucking guest.

As much fun as it was to show off and prove to everyone around you that you were a Disney-insider by using the lingo when you *weren't* working, I tried my best to avoid it, after hearing firsthand on many occasions how the practice could go from amusing to obnoxious in very little time at all.

Don't believe me? Sit next to some off-duty cast members on the monorail someday and see if you're not ready to toss them overboard after hearing a conversation the likes of...

"Last night's EMH sucked. We had to E-Stop twice. But, to make up for it, our Lead let us ride TSM, and I totally high-scored."

"No fair. I was working Stands West across from Pecos and got extended because we were at capacity and Spectro was running. At least I got a GSF for replacing a guest's turkey leg when he dropped it in the river on his way to TSI.

Yep, something about a loud and proud round of competitive cast speak always inspired (still does) fantasies of launching the offenders in question right outta their cozy little seats on the Mark VI and into 7SL upon exiting the Contemp on the way from the TTC to MK. Enough to make ya wanna V, know what I mean?

Back to the Magic Kingdom, and the mysterious underground city that lies beneath. That's probably the second most-asked question I get when I tell people I worked for Disney: "Are there really underground tunnels?" If I was one of the aforementioned monorail-passenger CMs (sorry, I can't stop), I would correct such egregious blasphemy and tell the asker, "Yes, there are Utilidors, but they are actually ground level, and MK is built on the second story." But I'm not, so I smile and say, "Sure are."

The *most* popular question, by the way, has definitely got to be, "Are those things air conditioned?"—in reference to the character costumes. "Has any costume anywhere, ever, in the history of the universe been air-conditioned?" is what I want to reply. But instead, I smile and say, "Sure are."

About those tunnels. We didn't do any real training to speak of in the Magic Kingdom, so it took me a while to get acquainted with the Utilidors. After thinking long and hard over the course of my Disney career, I decided the most accurate way to describe the distinct smell of the pixie-dusted passageways was a mix between freshly baked bread and rotting garbage, with a hint of that subtle smell that comes out of your vents, right when you turn the heat on in your car. And just a smidge of damp cave. Meanwhile, cast member radio and golf-cart horns was what you *heard*. Oh, and the rumble and rattle of the overhead trash disposal system. 1970s-era signage and colors, along with food shipments on forklifts, is what you *saw*. The electronic time clocks at the entrance/exit of the main corridor, and the complimentary hand-sanitizer pumps throughout, are what you *touched*. As far as *taste* goes, I'd say we're pretty much back to that whole bread-garbage-vent-cave thing. The stuff was thick. Like, go-home-and-your-pants-still-smell-like-Utilidors thick. The only safe-zone was Costuming, simply because the laundry smell overwhelmed any nostril that came within a few feet of the entrance. It's not exactly the fresh-laundry smell that made you wanna snuggle up in your warm PJs, fresh out of the dryer, but it beat bread-garbage-vent-cave.

The design of the tunneled backstage area posed some challenges. First, the commuting process was kind of a nightmare. Cast members were made to park their cars in an employee lot, affectionately known as West Clock—which, by the way, featured its own smaller costuming department—before they were transferred by company bus to the mouth of the Utilidors. Sounds easy enough, but because the Magic Kingdom was the biggest of the parks—in terms of employed cast members—the lines at West Clock could get absolutely outrageous. It wasn't uncommon to wait behind two or three buses' worth of people during the morning rush. And, at closing, when the entire kingdom was released at roughly the same time, the wait-time might as well have been another shift.

Another challenge—for me, at least—was finding my way around. Yes, it was a fairly straightforward design plan: a circular tunnel system with a main corridor cutting through the middle. But the sheer number of rooms, offices, stairways, elevators and other offshoots gave me problems as a newbie. Part of it could have been because we avoided the park, for the most part, during training: there wasn't really the time or room in MK for cast members that didn't already know what they were doing...especially when it came to characters. I also was rarely scheduled there afterward. It was my least-frequented park, and I only ever played two characters there: Goofy and Woody.

My first introduction came when I was scheduled for a half-day Goofy shift in Frontierland. I was thrilled to see my cowboy get-up as I collected my costume that morning: jeans, checkered shirt, western-style tie, and big ol' ten-gallon hat. Turned around in the Utilidors, I didn't even try to find warm-ups. I skipped and set out on the long walk, black bag on my back, through the tunnels. After asking a cast member for directions, I was pointed toward the elevator which would bring me up to Frontierland.

I was paired with Donald—coonskin-capped Donald, at that—and our off-set location was a second-story room hidden by the western-town façade that lined the main street running through the fictional boom town. The first thing I noticed, as I settled into the changing area, was how old everything looked—compared to the other parks, that is. I loved it, though. The vintage vibe of the walls, pictures, and even furniture—plus, you could look out the window and see the "roofs" of the Frontierland sets—made me feel like I was a part of the Walt Disney World of old. I imagined the thousands of other Goofys that had passed in and out of that room in the last four decades, and I felt as if I were a part of something really special.

The good feelings were diminished slightly when a headless Donald peeked around the corner to see if I was ready for our first set.

This particular duck was a fast-talking Puerto Rican woman who had bid the location and made it clear she had no tolerance for newbies. I soon found out that her abrasive nature extended to guests, as well. She had a thing about hitting kids in the face with the tail of her coonskin cap. She also did this weird thing where she'd stuff the tail into Donald's beak, and then, when a kid tried to pull it out, she'd grab the arm of the kid, while stomping loudly with a big webbed foot, and scare him/

her absolutely senseless. Two kids in our first set alone started bawling after being frightened by the Duck's cruel game and had to be ushered away by their parents without any photos or autographs.

She had one word to say about it once we'd returned upstairs. "Brats."

I had even less to say and popped my headphones in.

Besides Donald—I was pretty used to those damn ducks by then—I really enjoyed the location, and worked there several more times. We greeted guests at the side of the street, with the river just to our backs, so it could get hot. But, as a sucker for Disney theming and architecture—especially the time-travel feel of the Frontierland boom town—you couldn't beat the view.

Still, it had nothing on my other Magic Kingdom mainstay, a few steps down the road in Adventureland, which happened to be my favorite set location of any of the four parks. No matter how many new attractions come and old ones go, for me, nothing will ever beat Pirates of the Caribbean. And what is the next best thing to setting sail with Cap'n Jack on the Spanish Main? Dressing up like a scurvy dog yourself and hanging out with guests close enough to the attraction entrance to still feel the air conditioning. (*Wait, there's no A/C in this costume?*)

I could barely believe my eyes when I checked my schedule for the upcoming week on a cast computer in the Utilidors and saw Pirate Goofy listed for a straight week of shifts. To be honest, I hadn't even realized such a shift existed. As a guest, I'd never seen my alter-ego anywhere near the attraction, let alone dressed in full-blown swashbuckler garb. I asked a manager about it and was told that it was more of a seasonal shift that they implemented from time to time to give guests an added experience and to help thin the attraction line itself.

I showed up to work that week at the Magic Kingdom in an extra-good mood. After packing my black bag with pirate-style knee breeches and a billowy, gold-satin shirt, along with boots, sash, vest, bandana, hoop earring, and eyepatch, I changed into basics and set sail for Adventureland. But not before I stopped in for my morning warm-ups; I was so excited about my good fortune that I even took the time to locate the workout room in the twists and turns of the tunnel innards. Considering Adventureland's location at the front of the park, and thus proximity to the main entrance of the Utilidors, I arrived at the set location in no time at all.

The off-set facility was a modular that sat just behind the walled gate to the left of the attraction. Inside, I giddily dressed in preparation of the day's first set. I was so enamored with the costume, I forgot to drink my morning Power-Ade. My character attendant was a friendly Hawaiian girl who found the unique accessories to be as much fun as I did. She was tickled to tie the sash, tighten the bandana on Goofy's head, strap on the eyepatch, and secure the earring—and even more pumped to hand over the last and best of the accessories: a small plastic pirate cutlass.

"No freaking way!" I said, as she jokingly bowed and offered the sword, as if from servant to king in medieval times. "Where'd this come from?"

"Costuming."

"How did I miss this?" I asked.

"They give them to attendants now; characters were breaking them all," she explained.

"Breaking them?"

"Swordfights. In the Utilidors."

"Ahh," I said with a look on my face admitting I'd probably have done the same on the way over, had the weapon been in my possession earlier.

As we readied to go out, my backup—the Goofy who would alternate sets with me—showed up at the door, black bag in hand. When he saw the full glory of the costume, he was blown away. He started walking circles around me, admiring every inch. "This. Is. Awesome."

"Wait," I said, then drew the sword from my sash in dramatic fashion.

He lost his mind. "I'm getting dressed right now."

I laughed. Normally, performers waited until the last possible second to don their hot costumes before a set. In fact, it usually took some prompting from a manager or attendant to pry them away from their phones, books, naps, or TV show.

Yes, many of the off-set locations had televisions. Performers who bid there generally controlled the content. Many brought in Disney movies to watch, while some simply fed their soap-opera addictions with the network programming. Those locations were the worst, as far as getting a performer to his/her set on time. Of course, managers weren't keen on such behavior, and so most had outlawed soaps, citing the racy plotlines as the cause, rather than the mesmerized cast members. Still, even if we'd had a television in that tiny modular outside Pirates, I guarantee it would have gotten far less attention than the novelty of the day's costume.

The set itself was a breeze—sometimes literally, as a refreshing gust of air conditioning would every so often make its way out of the propped-open attraction doors and into my mouth screen. I was positioned only a few feet from the line, in full shade under the fort, with a backdrop of pirate props, mainly piles of loot and treasure. Though there was a steady stream of guests to greet, I signed few autographs and rarely posed—at least formally—for pictures. Having blades of their own—and for many, eyepatches and makeup, thanks to the nearby Pirates' League experience—most kids simply wanted to swordfight the Goof. I happily obliged. In an extra careful, non-violent Disney way, of course. People couldn't get enough of Pirate Goofy—guy wearing the mask included.

When my set ended, I skipped off to the backstage area, sword raised high in hand, high-fiving guests as I went. I entered the modular to find my backup racing around the room, terrorizing his attendant with his own sword. The two of them were laughing and having a great time. She didn't even have to coax him outside. At the first sight of me, he bolted out the door, eager to get on set. I had a seat and was about to remove my head, but realized I was enjoying my pirate experience too much and so decided to stay in costume even through my break. I placed my sword back under my sash, took a good look at myself in the full-length mirror on the wall, and headed back outside.

There was a thick layer of brush to the side of the modular. I walked the length of the greenery and eventually noticed a small path which cut inward. I took a few steps down it and realized it widened slightly as it wound its way around some small trees. I continued slowly and stopped altogether when I picked up the sound of chanting in the distance. I recognized it immediately, and my heart started to beat a little faster. I picked up the pace and in no time found myself at river's edge, smack dab in the middle of the Jungle Cruise. I suddenly heard the sound of a skipper's crackling radio voice and ducked behind a tree, just as a boat full of guests rounded the corner into view. I remained hidden, and watched and listened until all heads and bad jokes had faded into the distance. I took a seat on the sloped bank, careful to keep myself out of view, and relaxed for a good twenty minutes, watching the boats pass by. When I figured my break was about up, I waited for a gap in the boat traffic and made my way back through the short stretch of jungle and up to the modular.

"Where were you?" my concerned attendant asked.

"Restroom."

She eyed my mouth screen suspiciously, then shrugged her shoulders. "Five minutes to set."

I made a habit out of jungle-boat watching and returned to my spot on the river bank after each set. It made for a shady and cool spot to relax, even despite being in full costume. And, of course, the view was one in a million. On my last break of the day, I even let my attendant in on the secret and asked her to snap a few posed pictures of me—sword drawn, of course—on the banks of the Jungle Cruise river. In the shifts that followed, I continued to have an absolute blast playing pirate and returned every time to my jungle hideaway to rest up between shifts. At one point, I even got so brave as to show my face—rather, Goofy's face—to a few younger guests traveling the river.

Their boat had just passed, and I noticed two pre-teen boys near the back, their eyes fixed in my direction. Maybe they'd spotted some of the brightly colored costume amongst the foliage. I slowly rose and drew my sword, then bounded out from behind the tree, plunging my cutlass through the air straight at them. Their eyes nearly popped out of their heads, and they began shouting and pointing. The whole of their boat spun around, but I was well out-of-sight behind the tree by the time they did. Their skipper even stopped mid-joke to see what all the commotion was about, but nobody was ever able to catch a glimpse of the strange and mysterious pirate-dog who was reputed to be seen in the heart of the jungle that day.

Each shift at Pirates was a special experience, and I'm thankful that I was scheduled there multiple times. I even had other Goofys who saw me pulling the pirate costume in the Utilidors pre-shift beg to swap shifts with me, and even offer to pay me a little something to do so. I did share the magic and ended up switching with one of them—a nice guy who I'd worked with before on occasion. I even told him about my secret break-spot in the jungle. He thanked me profusely for trading and texted a steady stream of photos to me throughout the day, documenting his stint as a pirate.

Obviously, character performers get slightly excited and obsessive over their costume selections—myself included—so, although it was sad when my days of pillaging and plundering gave way to a string of morning shifts at Disney's Hollywood Studios, there was some consolation to be found in *their* costuming department. While I may not have been able to wear the outfits themselves, I had nearly just as much fun walking the aisles of Stormtrooper helmets and armor. Like so many others, I've always been a huge Star Wars fan and seeing, touching, and inspecting the spot-on costume replicas from the classic film series was a highlight of my time at Disney in and of itself. I'm not ashamed to say that I tried on the Stormtrooper mask nearly every time I worked at the Studios. On days when I was feeling especially nostalgic, I'd put on the Darth Vader mask piece by piece, humming the "Imperial March" as I did. Or, if none of the costuming cast members were looking, I'd throw on the Chewbacca head and do a Wookie-call in the mirror. The nature of that particular mask—extensive hair that needed brushing and regular maintenance—meant it was kept in a special location, separate from the other heads, which made it a little harder to access. Still, I took my chances and was able to sneak a "wear" now and again.

At the Studios, I only worked the "Hat shift," as it was called, in the Goofy role. Back when the despised-by-Disney-park-purists Sorcerer's Hat fronted the Chinese Theater at the end of Hollywood Boulevard, a line of classic characters—usually the Fab Five—would appear in the general vicinity for meet-and-greets throughout the day. Hat shifts never proved overly exciting and were typically predictable for the most part. The dressing room was large and chaotic, as it hosted character performers from several locations. I was often one of the only *guys* in the whole place, per usual. The conversation of the room generally centered on that week's episode of *Glee* (anything from "I'm so learning that mash-up," to "Kurt is my *boo*," to "I met Lea Michelle at an audition once, and she's a total bitch"), while I silently prepped for my set.

On the walk out to the Hat, characters would be mobbed by guests, who would get scolded by attendants, who would later be reprimanded by managers for not protecting their characters, after which, characters would be chewed out by attendants for dawdling and allowing guests to accumulate—those same guests who, no matter how fast you walked or how hard you tried to avoid it, would mob you anyway, and who would then get scolded yet again by attendants, who would later be reprimanded...and so on. I was indifferent to Goofy shifts at the Studios: they weren't my favorite, but they weren't the worst thing in the world, either. Out of all four parks, I visited the Studios the least...while in the dog-suit, that is. Thanks to the next character to appear on my work schedule, I ended up spending more time there than anywhere else on property. But, we'll get to that shortly...

While I'd been a Goofy fan growing up, "playing" him day in and day out over the course of a few years ensured that he came to occupy a special place in my heart. Tough as it was sometimes, whether the uncomfortable costume, the long hours, annoying guests or coworkers, I'll always count it an honor to have walked a mile in those giant, floppy clown shoes, to have received permanent neck damage from that mile-high hat, and to have looked out on the world for a period of time through that buck-toothed mouth screen.

Goof, I tip my hat to you, now and always. And not just any hat, but a very special one that no longer sits boxed on the top shelf of my closet. A hat that hangs two-eared, long-snouted, loud and proud from the corner of my headboard for all to see (but mostly me) who I was...and who, deep down, I still am.

CHAPTER FOUR

The Superhero

After a long stint of Goofy shifts, I was surprised to find a last-minute revision to my schedule one morning before work at Hollywood Studios: *Costume Fitting*. I was intrigued, and asked the scheduler at Character Base about it. After flipping through some paperwork, he told me that I was being fitted for Bob.

"Great!" I told him, and took a seat in one of the armchairs in the lounge area, where all incoming character performers and attendants stop to get their coffee or their morning news fix before scattering off to their various set locations. *Bob?* I thought. *As in Bob the Builder?* I'd seen him doing meet-and-greets at Playhouse Disney. But what a letdown: going from Goofy, a member of Disney's Fab Five, to a lame cartoon construction worker that had been popular with preschoolers for about five minutes.

A character attendant I recognized from a previous shift had a seat next to me. She started making small talk while she sipped her coffee. "You at Hat today?" she asked.

"No, I've got a fitting."

Her eyes lit up. "Really? Who?"

"Bob the Builder," I said, trying but failing miserably to match her excitement.

She looked at me skeptically. "Whaaaa?"

"Yep, I asked about it."

"There's not even a Bob the Builder *character*," she said, getting riled up from the mixture of caffeine and controversy.

"Uh-huh," I said matter-of-factly, "At Playhouse..."

She interrupted me. "That's *Handy Manny*!"

I shut my mouth and thought for a moment. *Damn.* I felt as stupid as the Dora wannabe from my training group. "Well, then...who...?"

"Go find out!" she said, practically pushing me out of my chair up to the desk.

It was embarrassing not to know things at Disney when everyone was walking around throwing out slang and acronyms like they were the second coming of Walt. Even still, I swallowed my pride and approached the scheduler to double-check on my shift. "Who did you say I was being fitted for?"

"Bob," he said, seeming slightly annoyed. The scheduling desk was a busy place, especially in the morning.

Even still, I followed up the answer with a request for clarification. Not fully wanting to let on that I was clueless, however, I stumbled awkwardly over my words. "Who...I mean, what exactly...like does he have a last name?"

"Mr. Incredible."

My eyes lit up: finally, a name I recognized.

"We refer to Mr. and Mrs. Incredible as Bob and Helen. Much easier."

Easier for who? I thought. *There they go with that damn Disney-speak again.*

I returned to my seat and informed my incredulous attendant-friend of the news. "Oh, *Bob*," she said, like it was the most obvious thing in the world. "Well, good luck, I hear he's a tough fit."

"What do you mean?"

"Almost nobody passes the fitting. Your measurements have to be spot on, 'cause the costume's a bitch."

Lovely, I thought to myself.

"Well," she raised her Styrofoam cup in a toast, "let's hope next time I see ya, you're a superhero."

I smiled and crossed my fingers.

She said goodbye, and I headed across the street to Costuming, where I checked out a single pair of basics, changed, and reported for my fitting.

An older female cast member, who looked and smelled as if she'd been working in the laundry room since the resort opened, greeted me and led me over to the "superhero" aisle of the room, where the costumes of Mr. and Mrs. Incredible—excuse me, *Bob and Helen*—as well as their buddy Frozone, hung in a long line of reds and blues.

She stopped in front of a Bob and turned around to face me with a sly grin. "Alright, this is my favorite part of the job."

"OK," I said, wondering where she was going with this.

"Strip!" she shouted, then immediately started cackling as long as she could before her laugh turned into a nasty smoker's cough.

This isn't awkward at all, I thought, as I dropped my shorts and removed my shirt right there in the middle of the aisle.

"I won't make you take those off," she said, grinning and pointing to my underwear.

I forced a laugh. "Thanks."

"First up: unitard," she said, removing a flesh-colored, full-body garment from a hanger.

I slipped into it, and she zipped me up in the back.

"Now, muscles." She handed over the next piece: another full-body suit, this one white with mesh pockets all over, holding a variety of padded and sculpted "muscles."

When I slipped my red, stretchy pair of superhero tights over the muscle suit, the pads turned my calves and thighs into Adonis-like tree trunks. The top half of the suit was a separate piece that came with a built-in "chest-plate" to make the performer's upper body appear disproportionate and cartoon-like to emphasize the character's physical strength even more. Once I slipped the very uncomfortable top over my head and made sure everything was situated in the right place—shoulders on top, biceps facing up, triceps down, pecs pointing forward—the attending cast member secured the piece with two straps, one running from the front and another from the back, that met and were fastened tightly together right in the nook of the crotch.

After fumbling with the snaps for a few moments, the old woman finally relinquished the delicate task. "I'll let you take it from here," she said with a laugh.

Tights layer—both tops and bottoms—securely in place, she pulled the next item of clothing from the rack: a pair of black superhero-style briefs. "Undies," she said, tossing them my way.

I slipped them on, and she asked me how everything felt. "My shoulders are going numb," I told her.

She tugged at my collar and shoved an arm down the back, pounding the muscle pads into place with her fist. Then, positioning herself squarely in front of me, she grabbed the sides of the large plastic chest-plate through the material and yanked. I lurched forward, as she did. "Better?" she asked.

I raised my arms and rotated my shoulders. "Actually, yeah," I said, feeling no pain or restriction.

"Go to the shoe room and pick out a pair of boots," she directed. "I'll get your mask ready."

I returned a few minutes later, walking a little taller—literally—in my oversized, calf-high, villain-stomping, superhero boots.

In her hands, the cast member held my new face, complete with blond plastic-molded hair, Zorro-style mask, and Leno-style chin.

I grabbed a skull cap and head-gear, and in no time at all, was admiring my new reflection in the mirror at the end of the aisle. The head was much different from the cumbersome hat-and-snout number to which I was accustomed. Bob's face was barely bigger than my own and fit snugly in place around my head. There was maybe an inch of space between my hair and the plastic above it—a far cry from the towering topper that extended more than a foot above the Goofy mask. This one was light and streamlined: no aching or straining in my neck. I felt ready for action.

"Last, but not least," she said, retrieving a pair of long, black, rubber gloves from a drawer on the nearest wall.

I slipped my left hand in and started pulling and stretching in an attempt to get the glove over my own skin, as well as the bulging forearm of the costume.

The cast member grabbed a bottle of baby powder. "Use this."

I poured liberally into each glove, and they went on smoothly. I clapped my hands and a poof of powder enveloped the two of us.

"Impressive," said the woman, starting to cough again.

When the particles cleared, there stood staring at me in the mirror a full-fledged, head-to-toe, real-life—well, almost real-life—superhero. I modeled my muscles and struck a few menacing poses. I turned to my pervy stylist and flashed her a thumbs-up.

She asked again how the costume felt, and if I was experiencing any discomfort.

I told her I felt great, and she scurried off to retrieve a manager for official approval, which meant I'd be cleared immediately to work Bob shifts.

The manager returned and inspected the fit, felt around some of the muscle pads, checked the tightness of the waistband, and asked me to demonstrate full-range of motion in my arms, legs, and neck. After walking a few circles around me, she began to nod her head in a satisfied fashion. "Wow, this costume was made for you."

Further evidence of this came when I checked my schedule the next morning and found nearly all my

Goofy shifts for the next two weeks had been switched to Bob shifts. Thus began my new residence at Hollywood Studios. I didn't mind a bit.

I'd loved the Studios growing up. During my teen years, when I backlashed slightly against the "kids' stuff" that the Magic Kingdom was made of, and sought out the sort of fast-paced thrills that only a Tower of Terror or a Rock 'n' Roller Coaster could provide, it was certainly my favorite of the four parks. Working there, I loved that I'd pass a couple Stormtroopers on my way in each morning, or that I did my warm-ups alongside the Power Rangers. Some mornings, after I'd prepped my costume and was killing time waiting for my pick-up, I'd cross the street to the backstage area of the Indiana Jones Stunt Spectacular and lean up against their spare, rubber boulder from the Golden Idol scene.

The Incredibles' meet-and-greets took place on the second level of what, at the time, was the Magic of Disney Animation. The downstairs break room was one of the larger and nicer on property, featuring a flat-screen TV, several leather couches, and a fridge that was always stocked with the blue stuff. The cast of characters that shared the building were a mix of classic Disney and Pixar. I always got a kick out of seeing feeble, gray-haired Carl from *Up* shuffle in with his walker, plop down on the couch, and pop off his head, only to reveal a pony-tailed girl inside. On days when Fantasmic was running, the room got even more crowded, as the character cast from the memorable nighttime show used it as a prep area themselves. Of course, there weren't enough seats to accommodate both the show and building casts, so it wasn't unusual to see Mary Poppins sitting on Genie's lap, or Maleficent and Pocahontas cross-legged on the floor chatting about life.

In addition to being supplied a wife, I also got my very own sidekick. Having a male co-worker was a nice change of pace; the Frozone character was tall enough that very few girls qualified for the role. Obviously, I had nothing against working with girls, but there's something about two little-boys-at-heart dressing up and playing "super-hero" that's just good fun. Of course, I was only paired with him on days when I was scheduled in Group 2—the switch-outs who spelled Mr. and *Mrs.* Incredible.

Helen was no slouch, though. The female performers who played her took the role very seriously and were always trying to be as authentic as possible when it came to Elastigirl's superhuman capabilities. I had several athletic co-workers who would flop down into full-on splits without warning while greeting a family, or maybe lift one leg high into the air, up and behind the head—like an extreme yoga pose—while the guests marveled and PhotoPass snapped away.

One particular Helen basically performed an all-out gymnastics routine over the course of any given set. She loved to dart around as fast as she could—a la her superhero alter-ego—both on set, and to and from set. The meet-and-greet location was one floor above backstage, so a lengthy set of stairs had to be used to travel between the two. The stairs were on set and were also used by guests. The missus and I usually played up our roles by walking the stairs arm-in-arm, perhaps stopping midway to give each other a loving smooch on the cheek. This Helen, however, would have none of that lovey-dovey stuff.

She'd bolt through the door onstage, frantically scanning the room, as if she was in hot pursuit of Syndrome. Guests jaws would drop and they'd hurry around for a picture (provided they hadn't been in the path of the flung-wide metal door she'd just burst through). I'd amble through after, all muscles and grins in what amounted to a comparatively flat and unexciting entrance. As soon as I'd get through the door, my over-eager partner would grab my hand and race me up the stairs—sometimes taking two at a time. When it was time to leave, she'd take off again, pulling me behind, down the stairs and through the backstage door in a flash. Guests and managers loved it; I hated it.

One afternoon, when she was dragging me off set in her usual fashion, she leapt down the first few stairs as I struggled to keep up.

At the same time, a guest on the other side of the room shouted my name.

I looked up and gave him a friendly wave. Taking my eyes off the ground for that split-second caused me to lose my footing; my giant, oversized boots didn't help matters.

Of course, Elastigirl had already taken another three stairs in the time it had taken me to look up and back down.

The tug of her arm jerked me forward and off-balance. I overcompensated and wobbled backwards, my free arm flailing out to the side, desperately trying to keep me upright. The toes of my boots went up, and I teetered momentarily on the raised heel-portion of the backs of my soles.

Elastigirl didn't stop.

With a jarring thud, I skidded down to the next step, my boot heels the only part of me touching the staircase. I prayed silently that my life would not end with a series of front flips down a set of stairs wearing tights and fake muscles in front of a paparazzi-like collection of cameras. Miraculously, I was able to stay upright, and I literally surfed down the dozen or so stairs on the backs of my boots, never once gaining control of my balance.

Oohs and *aahs* echoed all over the room, as my feat warranted the praise of all who'd witnessed it.

At the bottom of the staircase, I nearly fell from the force of the ride, as my boots finally touched down on flat, solid ground, but again, I was somehow able to re-main standing after only a few stumbling steps. As soon as I had my bearings again, I disgustedly shook free of my pretend-wife, who had no idea what had just taken place.

I hoped the guests gathered around believed my stunt to be intentional—just a cool "superhero" trick that I busted out from time to time for my fans. Two adolescent boys, however, in absolute hysterics over my flub, dashed all such notions I held of maintaining my dignity.

Elastigirl tried to grab my arm once more as she streaked for the door.

I batted her hand away and walked bitter and alone back to the dressing room with a single thought running through my hung head: *I miss Frozone.*

He and I were back together soon enough. Working the shift so often, I got to know the three or four guys who were tall enough to play the character pretty well. One of them had bid the location, so he was there five days a week. He was a beanpole, white as a ghost, with glasses and short, greasy hair. He'd formerly worked as a librarian. I found the oddity of this guy transitioning from a quiet life of books to daily performances in a chaotic theme park as a Samuel L. Jackson-voiced superhero quite funny. I couldn't help but smile when I saw him mornings in Character Base fixing up his coffee with eight or nine creams and sugars, every cowlick on his head standing straight up, while he caught that day's weather report on the tube.

Another of my Frozones, who filled in from time to time on the librarian's days off, was a guy about my age, dead-set on delivering an authentic experience to guests. Thankfully, his didn't involve any acrobatics—or stairs. One of his favorite tricks, though, was to retrieve an ice cube from the freezer in the break room and tuck it into his rubber glove as we were leaving to go out on set.

Then, he'd burst through the door on set, attracting as much attention as he could. Guests would crowd around with their cameras and autograph books, and he'd lead them over to the drinking fountain located on the lower level of the building. He'd motion for a guest to press the button to turn the fountain on, while he subtly tilted his arm and slid the ice cube out into the palm of his other hand. As the water spouted up, he'd raise his hands dramatically like a sorcerer and thrust them towards the stream, as if he were casting a spell. He'd then pass his hand quickly under the water and flip it over to reveal the ice cube that he'd just "frozen" with his trademark superpower. The crowd loved it and would break into applause as he handed the ice over to some bewildered young fan and then dash off to the set location.

This is the same guy who, as Goofy, would break into the "perfect cast" (a la *The Goofy Movie*) at least once a day on set. As Woody, he'd tuck a rubber snake into his cowboy boot, and at some point during a guest-interaction, whip it out for a laugh that referenced the pull-string toy's famous line: "There's a snake in my boot!" He ended up discontinuing the latter practice after one of his co-worker buddies got canned by management in the middle of a shift for pulling the same stunt.

As Mr. Incredible, I didn't have any such tricks up my sleeve, or hidden in any other parts of my costume. I suppose my biggest claim to fame was my "autograph." Because of the massive chest-plate tucked into the front of the costume, it was impossible for me to bring my arms close enough together for my hands to meet. Therefore, signing an autograph wasn't an option. Disney's solution was to give Mr. I a rubber stamp that did the job—only one hand required—as well as a special podium where the autograph books were set and stamped, and an attendant to hold the book open while said stamping took place. The stamp itself was self-inking, meaning it was one of those plastic numbers that contained a mechanism which required a forceful push in order to flip the stamp face from its upward inking position down toward the paper into stamping position.

My training buddy, who frequently played the role of Buzz Lightyear, was also required to make use of the high-tech art of stamping, since the plastic fingers of his space-ranger gloves didn't get along well with pens. He and I got to talking one day about how we felt slightly cheated by the signing process. We complained that we weren't able to add any real personal touch to autographs. The long process of a guest handing their autograph book over to the attendant, who in turn placed it on the podium, where it was quickly stamped, then removed, then handed back, often made for a dry, mechanical interaction. So, we came up with a solution to add a little more fun and flair back into the mix, and started turning autograph signings into a show in and of themselves. Though interactions took a bit longer and made for a little more work, the results were totally worth it. Guests loved our solution. Buzz and I would tell each other the stories and even get our attendants to film a few of the interactions per shift, so we could compare notes and try to best the other with our moves.

A typical performance would begin with me confronting the guests, bowing, and taking their autograph book from them. I'd then lead them over to the podium, where I would lay the book face up, smoothing the pages down to ensure it stayed flat and open. Next, I'd carefully place the plastic stamp on the part of the page to be "signed," then leave it be. After pausing dramatically and taking a few exaggerated deep breaths, I'd launch into a ridiculously elaborate routine—something of a Tai Chi demonstration—with a good twenty seconds of slow, deliberate stances and poses. Just when I'd mesmerized the guests and their expectancy was sky high, I'd bust out a lightning-fast spin move and karate chop the hell out of the stamp, leaving one *Mr. Incredible* on the page and countless looks of awe and admiration on the faces of all those around.

The show never got old. Well, at least to my buddy and me it didn't. It may very well have to the attendants who had to sit through multiple demonstrations per set, or had to explain to management why we were going through so many stamps (it seemed they were only built to last about a day's worth of karate chopping each). I could tell Frozone was jealous, especially ice-cube guy. But, with no chest-plate, and full use of his hands and fingers, the old boy was stuck scrawling like the rest of them. One of my blue-suited partners, however, absolutely ate it up. He praised me for the routines after every set, and texted and called all his friends, trying to coax them into coming over to Studios to see Kung-Fu Bob.

In real life, he was a blond-haired surfer type and the only other straight male inside the animation dressing room on any given day. He had a thing for Pocahontas, and so tried his best to trade shifts and finagle his way into the super-suit whenever Fantasmic was running. Since John Smith and all the princes were in love with each other, Poca (her slang Disney name) was all about the attention and flirted shamelessly with Surfer Boy in between sets. Because of the close quarters that resulted on Fant-days, hormones were usually raging anyways.

I remember returning one day to the hustle and bustle of the break room after a long shift and ripping off my mask and upper body, just before a towel was thrown my way. I caught it and saw Mary Poppins sitting seductively on the leather couch. She was staring down my sweaty body with a *sex-pi-ali-docious* look in her eye.

"Not just *incredible* on the outside," she said playfully.

I smiled politely and wiped my face.

"Practically perfect in every way," she continued.

Thankfully—or not—her advances were interrupted by a horny, gay Genie who'd been eyeing me for the past few weeks. "Nuh-uh, girl," he shouted to Mary from across the room, where he'd been watching the interaction, "He's mine. Come over here and sit on Genie's lap, Bobby-boy."

I rolled my eyes, packed my bag, and got out of there before he or Poppins could grant me any wishes. *Ahh, Fant-days.*

Surfer Boy, on the other hand, welcomed all the attention he could get from his Indian princess. Just before our last set of the shift—and after a long day of break-time flirting—he turned to me as we readied our costumes and said, "I'm gonna be hittin' that before the weekend." He nodded in Poca's direction.

She was too far away to hear, but knew she was being talked about and gave a sly smile.

Genie just happened to walk by and noticed Surfer Boy staring. "Put your tongue back in your mouth, Fro-Yo," he said a bit jealously.

I quickly put on my mask to avoid having to contribute to the conversation.

Our set went off without a hitch, and we were just about to call it a night when one last family approached. Frozone and I both looked to the attendant to see if she'd deny the guests or allow one last meet-and-greet.

She looked to us and mouthed, "Yes or no?"

Frozone immediately gave a thumbs-up and waved the family—a mother and her twenty-something son—toward us. He'd been in an extra-rowdy mood all set, probably thanks to his making "progress" with Poca.

It only took a few moments to realize that the son was a very special individual. He couldn't speak and communicated with the use of some basic sounds and hand signals. He had some difficulty walking and was assisted by his mother, who explained to all of us that the young man was a very big fan of The Incredibles and had been waiting all day to meet his heroes.

"Frozone is his absolute favorite," she said, patting me on the arm, as if to console me.

My sidekick—the least popular of the two of us when it came to meet-and-greets—perked up at the news and made a beeline to the young man, arms outstretched to embrace his admirer.

"Yeah, I'm afraid he's got a little crush," his mother confided to me, just before she looked up to see Frozone about to give her son a big hug. "Oh, I wouldn't..." she began.

But it was too late.

Arms apart, Frozone had left himself exposed and vulnerable.

The young man grabbed the superhero's plastic head firmly with both hands and pulled hard, jerking Frozone forward and up against him. Before anyone knew what was happening, a long, wet tongue shot out and started French-kissing ol' Fro-Yo. Up, down, and all around.

I watched as Frozone tried helplessly to pull away. As he did, however, his mask began to come off. He stopped immediately and carefully stepped forward in order to avoid breaking the cardinal rule of character-dom: destroying the magic by showing your face onstage. He simply had no choice but to lean in and take it like a champ. And, that's exactly what he did...for a solid two minutes. I'm not exaggerating.

The mother tried to intervene, but the lip-locked son was having none of it. He was in the *zone*—literally— and wasn't about to let up.

Unfortunately for all involved, the son soon enough started making loud, moaning sounds to go along with the tonsil hockey. The scene became almost unbearable. None of us knew what to do.

I wanted to gouge my eyes out...both pairs.

The mother had begun to yell at her son, but to no avail.

Frozone was frozen, due to the very real possibility of his being de-masked on-set.

The attendant, meanwhile, was pleading with the young man to unhand her character, which only seemed to egg him on—that whole forbidden love thing, I suppose.

Finally, once my suffering sidekick had been good and manhandled, kissed like he'd never been and never would be again—not even if Poca got a hold of him—the nightmare ended.

The young man stepped away with the biggest smile I'd ever seen on a guest's face, wiped the drool from his chin, and started giggling uncontrollably.

As bad as I felt for Frozone, I found it difficult not to do the same.

I had to give it to my partner-in-crime-fighting, though; he somehow managed to maintain his composure, and ever the gracious victim, stood there waving goodbye to the pair until they'd gone. Still, I'm pretty sure I saw him flinch at one point when his kissing buddy took a step toward him, as if he might go another round.

As soon as the three of us stepped off-stage, our attendant began apologizing profusely.

Frozone whipped off his head and inspected the face. "That's gonna have to be disinfected."

"Dude, I'm so sorry," I told him. "If I coulda done something, I woulda."

"Yeah," he said, staring off into space, as if he were reliving the horror in his mind.

We walked down the hallway to the break room in an awkward silence, all thinking about what we'd just witnessed.

As we entered the room and began changing, Poca noticed our somber faces and called out from her couch-seat, "Welcome back, boys."

We barely acknowledged the comment, and began rounding up our gear for the golf-cart ride back to base.

Not coping well with being ignored, Poca rose and approached. "How was your set?"

"Well..." I began.

"Great!" said Frozone, promptly cutting me off. The sight of Poca standing before him seemed to snap him out of his catatonic state and brought some of the color back to his face. "It was...ya know...the usual."

She smiled.

I packed the last of my costume into my black bag and headed toward the door, patting my sidekick on the back as I went, "See ya outside, man."

"So, you wanna get together tonight or what?" I heard him say in a lowered voice, as I walked away.

"Mm-hmm," responded Poca.

"Haven't you had enough action for one night?" I called back, as I exited the room, leaving my smooth-talking partner to explain.

The door closed to the sound of our character attendant spitting out her gulp of Power-Ade, while a confused Poca began demanding answers.

I was still close enough to hear Genie, who'd apparently just caught wind of the drama, let loose a shocked—but excited—scream. "Fro-Yo, you naughty boy, you."

The only real problem *I* had with a guest during my run as Mr. Incredible was of the exact *opposite* nature. At the time, Disney-Pixar's *Toy Story 3* was a few weeks from hitting theaters, so it was announced to all of us in Animation one afternoon that we'd be displaced for a couple days. The interior of the building was to receive an update in the form of a brand-new set location to help introduce the park's newest character, Lotso.

Every group of characters was reassigned to various locations around the park. For the Incredibles, this meant we'd be forced to leave the air conditioning (actually, with the amount of guests packed inside the animation building at any given time, the temperatures were sometimes worse inside than out) and set up shop outdoors, next to a large planter that was positioned near the exit of the building's theater. The short film inside would still run during the refurbishment, but guests would be made to exit immediately afterward, rather than ushered into the larger, open section of the building where meet-and-greets took place, per standard operating procedures.

The location actually proved to be a lot easier than our regular setup. Hardly anyone visited the film—even when the building wasn't under construction—so the guest-flow was minimal. Since we were somewhat tucked away on one side of the building, guests roaming that section of the park couldn't really see us, either. We did a lot of standing around and chatting with our character attendants for a few days. Ice-Cube Frozone also got some more practice in on the perfect cast, and I honed a few new stamp/chop moves. Every time the automatic doors from the theater would creak open, we'd snap to attention, ready to welcome any outbound guests. Usually, there weren't any. Every so often, an older couple would slowly emerge, maybe wave and smile as they passed, showing no real interest in a full-blown interaction.

Things remained quiet until midway through the second day in our improvised set location, when the doors opened to the sound of a screaming boy, probably twelve or thirteen years in age. He'd been fighting with his parents; I caught just the tail-end of a very impolite directive aimed at mom and dad, which contained a certain four-letter verb. He was a few steps ahead of them, looking as if he were planning on leaving them behind.

I was standing about twenty feet away, facing the theater doors. Frozone and our attendant were ten feet off to my left.

When the little brat saw me, hellfire ignited in his eyes, and he took off running at full-speed straight toward me.

At first, I thought he might just be overly excited to meet me, and so I took a step in his direction. When I saw in his deranged face that this was not the case, I froze in my tracks. He was coming fast, and I didn't have much time to think. Of course, had we not been at the Most Magical Place on Earth, I could have easily just thrown up a clothesline. But, considering how any sort of contact—even self-defense—would likely bring about a lawsuit, I resolved to simply stand my ground, arms at my side, free and clear of any assault charges.

His arm—*fist*, rather—did not have any qualms, however, about physical contact. As he drew within punching distance, he did just that. He wound up and planted one with all the force and momentum of his barreling body, square in my gut.

Thirteen years of age or not, when anyone lets you have it in the stomach, you're gonna feel it. And feel it, I did. I reeled backwards, gasping for breath.

He started laughing maniacally.

His parents, who'd been trailing along slowly—probably hoping to lose their gem-of-a-son—saw what had happened and started yelling.

It only made the kid prouder of what he'd done.

I fought the urge to throw up in my mask—or to retaliate. There was nothing I could do, not even reprimand the little bastard. *Or, was there...*

His parents were still several steps away, their weary faces betraying how *thrilled* they were to have to engage in another shouting match with their progeny.

I steadied myself and bent over slightly, so that the two of us were eye-level. Cockily, I raised my glove and pointed at my chest, daring him to strike again.

The fire in his eyes raged, and he took the bait. He coiled and let fly an even harder blow than the first.

A loud, hollow thud echoed through the humid Florida air.

Punchy fell onto the cement, howling. He grabbed his fist and looked up toward his parents with watery eyes. "It's broken," he kept saying over and over in a weepy voice.

His parents had no sympathy. They grabbed him by the injured paw and jerked him to his feet.

He screamed from the pain and started to full-on cry.

With a grin to match that on the mask I was wearing, I adjusted my rock-solid chest-plate, pulled up my briefs, and walked with a slight swagger back over to Frozone and our attendant. Subtle fist-bumps all around.

Sometimes, due to the nature of the costume, I hurt guests I *wasn't* trying to, as well. In this regard, Mr. Incredible's gloves were incredibly dangerous. They were not your run-of-the-mill rubber gloves that you could pick up amidst the cleaning supplies in a local store. They were custom designed for longevity and of a thick, glossy consistency that clung to human hair like glue.

On more than one occasion, I'd pose with my arm around the side or shoulder of a female guest whose long locks made contact with my gloved hand. The strands would plaster themselves onto the rubber, so that after the photo was taken and we all broke the pose, their heads would be yanked along for the ride as I returned hand to side. Of course, they all cried out in pain whenever it happened, which got the attention of the whole line—sometimes, building. I'd then be left to explain to the masses—but especially their husbands, boyfriends, or fathers—without the use of any words mind you, why I'd just given some poor girl whiplash...a walk in the park, though, compared to the shame and utter humiliation of doing it to a lady with a wig. The low point of my days as a superhero.

After the refurb on the animation building, the break room got even more crowded. Lotso was absolutely massive—one of the biggest characters on property. I'm talking girth, not popularity-wise—although the guests adored him. All of us Animation regulars were slightly bitter. Not because he was grabbing all our attention and shortening our own meet-and-greet lines; we were actually grateful for that. But because his hastily constructed set location left the whole place reeking of paint and glue. The building was stuffy and poorly ventilated as it was. Disney's rush to resume normal operations after the refurb left no time even for the paint to dry—the walls were literally still sticky. That's to say nothing of the few days' worth of toxic fumes that were yet to dissipate. Most guests wouldn't even try to endure it: after five minutes and most likely a migraine, they'd hightail it out. Unfortunately, none of *us* had a choice. One of our character attendants actually passed out onstage from the fumes.

Bob and Helen—our switch-outs—were in the middle of a set at the time. Frozone and I were relaxing, sitting on a couch, chatting over Power-Ade, when the break room door was practically kicked down by Mr. Incredible. In true superhero fashion, he stood there like something off a comic-book cover: legs spread, head held high, with the unconscious college-age-male attendant cradled within his bulging arms.

The room gasped in shock at the sight.

"Bob!" yelled my counterpart.

I stood up.

"I've gotta get back to set," he cried. *Not only a superhero, but a model cast member, as well.*

Still in costume—minus the head—I ran over and took the lame body in my own arms.

In dramatic fashion, Bob #1 saluted the room.

His fellow characters broke into applause over the heroic display.

In a flash, he was gone.

All attention then turned to Bob #2, everyone wanting to see if I could finish the job and save the day.

I slipped out the door, victim in hand, and instead of going left down the hallway toward onstage, I took a right toward the outdoor exit. I yelled for Frozone to grab a bottle of Power-Ade and follow me out.

My sidekick—along with the rest of the room—came flooding behind.

One of the character attendants shouted, "I'm calling 911," as we made our way out of the building.

I set the young man down on a patch of grass next to the sidewalk.

After a few moments in the fresh air, he began to come to.

I called for the Power-Ade and made him take some small sips.

He finally felt well enough to sit up.

The crowd of characters surrounding started joking with him about how he'd been rescued by superheroes. "They saved your life!" somebody said in an over-exaggerated tone. "Mr. Incredible, you're my hero!" said another in a high-pitched, little-girl voice. We all had a good laugh, and were able to keep his mind off how terrible he was feeling until the ambulance arrived.

The paramedics checked him out and hooked him up to an IV. They said he would be fine, but wanted to take him down to the hospital just to be safe.

Later in the day, management came into the break room to announce that he was in fact OK and would be back to work in a few days. They gave a shout-out to me and the other Bob for our roles in helping to protect the fine citizens of Animation.

I rose to my feet to acknowledge their gratitude and gave the room the least cheesy smile and wave that I could for a guy dressed in a spandex suit and tighty-blackies.

A few days later, the fallen attendant returned and thanked me in person. He wasn't in the greatest of moods, however, having just learned that Disney wasn't taking any responsibility in the matter and refused to pay for the ambulance or any medical treatment.

"They said it was my fault," he told me. "Didn't eat a big enough breakfast."

"That's bullshit."

"That's Disney," he said.

In the story of Mouse and men...Mickey wins every time.

CHAPTER FIVE

The Soldier

After saving the world—or at least the life of a co-worker (okay, maybe just the *dignity* of a co-worker)—the next logical step was to enlist. In Andy's toy-soldier army, that is. I'm talking about Andy of *Toy Story* fame, of course, and those lovable little green men that are always busy pulling off rescue missions of their own throughout the films. Becoming a soldier was actually a happy accident that all came about because of a blessed five-letter word that appeared without warning on my schedule one week—a word that all character performers came to know and love, and looked expectantly for, as each new block of shifts came through the cast scheduling system: *spare*.

"Spare" meant you were an extra for the day. It meant you didn't have any formal assignment, but instead got to hang around doing any grunt work Character Base may have until someone called in sick, *got* sick mid-shift, or became generally fed up with children and wanted to go home.

I reported for duty at Studios on my first "spare" day, having no idea what to expect. I had to have my old buddy, the scheduler, explain things to me once again. Delighted by the prospect of a sort of "grab-bag" day—not knowing when my name might be called for any number of characters—I hung around base for a while, running paperwork here and there, drinking some coffee, going outside and leaning up against the Indiana Jones boulder. Eventually, the time came when the base had no more errands for me to run and no shift gaps to fill. No one had called in sick, gotten sick, or had a complete meltdown.

"How tall are you?" asked the scheduler. Satisfied with my response, he nodded. "You're in the army now."

I was immediately deployed to Costuming to get my green on.

The Green Army Man (or GAM, as it's referred to in character land) costume was a blast. And, by far, the easiest of any costume in all of Wardrobe. There was a jacket and pair of pants—stiff and plastic and green—to provide the necessary aesthetic for a toy soldier. A utility belt with a canteen hanging from it; a helmet; green army boots fastened to custom-cut pieces of wood to imitate the solid base of the iconic toys; and, of course, the mask...which everyone loved.

The mask was a simple metal face-plate with indentations for the eyes, nose, mouth, and curvature of cheeks and chin. It was made of a mesh-like design—so the performer retained visibility through it—over which a stretchy see-through green material was laid to achieve that *face-but-no-face* look of the toys. The best part, however, was that the face itself—according to Costuming—was cast from the original Han Solo Carbonite Chamber mold, so that essentially all of the Green Army Men were running around wearing Harrison Ford's face. Perhaps it was just another one of those Disney urban legends, but I chose to believe it. It did appear to be true by the look of the thing (at least I convinced myself it was). Even if it was a complete sham, I had no problem in this case subscribing to the ignorance-is-bliss theory, since it meant I got to wear my celebrity idol's face on mine.

There were a few other major perks to the GAM gig, the set location being one. Of course, the Toy Soldiers were an exclusive feature of Pixar Place, but the cool part was that we had *all* of Pixar Place. Two or three

soldiers would go out at a time as free-roaming characters—one of the only roles on property where this was
allowed. No character attendants, backdrop, or formal
line. Nothing. You were out in the field on your own.
I took advantage of it.

I hid around corners and scared guests; belly crawled
along the pavement; ducked behind trash cans to avoid
enemy fire; marched the length of the street and back,
saluting passersby as I went. I loved it, and guests loved
it. With the breathable costume and our generous helping of freedom, the sets always flew by, and we were back
to the break room in no time, talking about how cool it
was living life with Harrison Ford's mug.

The break room was another plus. It was nothing more
than a closet, really, but the Buzzes and Woodys with
whom we shared it were always good for a laugh, *and* it
was right next door to the Great Movie Ride. You could
get there through a backstage shortcut, walk around behind the scenes of the attraction, or even hang out in
their much-larger and much-nicer break room.

During my first spare shift, I made friends with a female
Buzz Lightyear who quoted movie lines from the 1990s
like it was her job. She was the one who first told me to
go check out the Great Movie Ride. "Beats this shithole,"
she said, trying to fit into her space-ranger suit without
busting her jet pack on the too-close-together walls.
"Plus, you can see Tom Hanks' autograph."

"What now?" I said, immediately intrigued. First
Harrison's face, now Tom Hank's autograph. Am
I in heaven?

"It's on the wall, backstage, behind the load-station,"
she said, stepping into a giant armored leg with one foot,
quoting *Toy Story* as she did. "To infinity and beyond!"

"On the *wall*?"

"Yep, with all the hands."

She went on to explain how all cast members who worked the attraction dipped their hand in paint and left a handprint behind on the backstage wall whenever they retired or were transferred. They would then sign their name underneath, as a way to leave a piece of themselves behind. Apparently, Mr. Hanks—though he obviously never worked there—was always a big fan of the attraction, heard about the tradition, and added his own hand and signature to the wall on a visit years ago.

I was skeptical. "Tell the truth," I said, shaking my head over the bogus story.

"You can't handle the truth!" she burst out, then added with a smile, "*Officer and a Gentleman.*"

"I know."

"But, for real."

"You're killin' me, Smalls," I said, joining in her game.

She nodded and smiled approvingly. "But, it *is* true; I'll take you there after my set."

"Alright," I said skeptically.

"Now, help me into my other leg."

I held the awkward bottom half of her costume in place, while she swung her leg up and in. Her other foot, already in a space-boot, scooted forward on the tile floor as she maneuvered, just enough to throw the whole operation out of whack. She lost her balance and fell in my direction, cracking her skull on the bone of my kneecap, then going down all the way to the floor face-first.

By the sound of the bone-on-bone impact—along with the fact that my knee felt like I might never be able to use it again—it seemed a concussion was a given. Maybe she was already dead. I knew one thing: I wasn't about to call an ambulance.

I reached down and shook her shoulder to see if she was conscious.

Her whole body started shaking uncontrollably.

She was bawling from the pain.

I couldn't see her face, but I was certain there'd be blood. I scrambled for the box of tissues on a nearby shelf and set them down next to her head.

She continued to shake and managed to ask between sobs, in broken sentences, what the tissues were for.

"The blood," I told her.

"Blood?" came a muffled reply.

"Or tears…"

She shook harder. "There's no…" She was having trouble getting the words out.

"What?" I said, leaning in.

"There's no…" She started to roll over.

Her bright red face came into view, and I suddenly saw she was in hysterics *laughing*, not crying.

"There's no crying in baseball," she finally got out.

"Huh?"

"*League of Their Own*," she said, laughing even harder.

"Oh my god."

Crisis averted, she finished dressing and made it out to her set on time. Immediately afterward, as promised, she led me through the shortcut to the back entrance of the Great Movie Ride's Wall of Hands. She had to search around for about thirty seconds before she located it among the hundreds there.

"How do you like them apples," she said. "*Good Will…*"

"I *know*," I interrupted. "Just like I know that is *not* Tom Hanks' signature."

"What do you mean?" she snapped, as if I'd just insulted her mother.

The handprint itself was tiny—almost like a girl's hand—while the signature looked as if a child had scribbled it there. It wasn't an "autograph," but simply the name written out in cursive. In *pencil* to boot.

"You're telling me that's how Tom Hanks—the biggest movie star in the world—signs his name. And uses a *pencil* to do it?!"

"But my trainer told me the whole story."

"*My* trainer told me our costumes cost $50,000. Come on, I've got a set."

We headed for our break room. She was too distraught for even a single movie quote the whole way back.

I kept giving her a hard time as I put my mask on and tucked the green scarf which covered it under my helmet. "I love my Harrison-face," I said, gloating over my much-cooler—and far less dangerous—costume.

"Your *what*?" she said with a bewildered look on her face.

"My Harr..."

"I heard you, but what's *that*?"

"Oh, Costuming used the same mold for this mask that was used to cast Han Solo's Carbonite Chamber."

She burst out laughing.

"What?"

"Who told you that?" she said, losing it.

"A cast member in Costuming."

"You're telling me that's Harrison Ford's face—the biggest movie star in the world—and that...and that..." She couldn't finish because she was laughing too hard.

I never believed another cast member rumor again.

Still, on days when I wasn't working with ol' Movie Lines, it *was* Harrison's face.

And I'm sure that on days when I was absent from the Pixar Place break room, Tom Hanks really did leave his chicken-scratch, tiny-ass handprint on that damn wall.

CHAPTER SIX

The Cowboy

I soon began spending even more time at Pixar, thanks to the advent of my fourth official character role in the scheduling system. Keeping it in the Toy Story family, I traded in my army boots for cowboy ones with *Andy* scrawled on the bottom. The set location for Buzz and Woody was a room at the far end of the Toy Story Mania building with an indoor queue and large picture windows allowing the guests outside to take pictures, wave, or make faces as they passed by.

While the GAM get-up had proved to be one of the easiest and most enjoyable of the costumes, Woody was a challenge. The costume wasn't overly heavy, nor did it entail an unusual amount of work to get into. It just never fit my body comfortably.

The main problem was the head. Whereas the rest of it was pretty straightforward—shirt, vest, neckerchief, pants, boots, and gloves—the head was of a different make and model than any that I'd encountered before. It was one solid piece of molded plastic, and similar to wearing a large bucket on your head. The sides of the heavy, hatted mask were designed to rest on the performer's shoulders for support—or, in my case, cut into the bones of my shoulders until they were a nice shade of bruise-purple. To make matters worse, the size and clumsiness of the head required that it be locked into place with straps. Once it was on, an attending cast member would have to reach up and under the plastic neck and buckle the straps—one extending downward from the inside of the head, one extending upward from the back of the costume—with a locking mechanism. It allowed for hardly any movement or rotation, being fastened tight to the collar of your shirt. If you've never experienced encasing your head in plastic and locking it down, so that only another human being can reach up and unlatch it from behind to let loose your seizing neck muscles and allow regular oxygen flow, let me tell you, it does wonders for your claustrophobia. Needless to say, I wasn't a huge fan.

The first few times I wore the costume, I was in major pain and had to talk myself down. In fact, the only time I ever used the SOS hand signal in the whole of my Disney career, was inside—and because of—the Woody head.

The character attendant had locked the head into place and pulled the straps extra tight, effectively pushing my head down into my body like an accordion, which greatly hindered my ability to move and breathe—let alone make magic. As I walked out onto set, I realized the awkward fit, and burning and tingling in the tops of my shoulders where the hard plastic edges were pressing into my flesh, would be far too much to handle for half-an-hour's time. I squirmed around in an attempt to find some kind of relief—to no avail. I started to breathe heavier and faster, growing nervous over the prospect of being stuck in that position for the length of an entire set. Buzz and the guests at the head of the line—a group of bratty kids who were busy fighting with one another over who got first dibs on a space-ranger hug—were entirely distracted, so I took the window of opportunity, wheeled around toward the character attendant, placed my left hand over Woody's eye, and shot my other high into the air.

As I did, the character attendant stepped forward to calm the quarreling kids and missed the signal.

I stood there for a few seconds, holding the position, wondering how much longer I could endure.

Some guests, strolling by the windows, saw my raised hand and thought I was waving at them. They waved back energetically.

I started hopping from boot to boot, trying to get the attendant's attention.

The guests thought I was playing some sort of game and mimicked my actions, even throwing their hands over their eyes as they jumped up and down in place.

Exasperated, I lowered both hands, took a few quick steps forward, and reached to tug the attendant's shirt.

As I did, one of the rambunctious kids grabbed the opportunity—and my hand—shook it wildly, then thrust an autograph book into it.

I tried to shake my head to indicate I wasn't able to sign mid-panic-attack, but my ability to do so was still locked securely in place. So, I ignored the guest for the time being and gave my attendant an annoyed slap on the arm with the autograph book.

The oblivious cast member, who was still playing peacemaker to the rowdy family, barely turned around. He caught a glimpse of the book out of the corner of his eye and retrieved something from his pants pocket. "Need a pen, Woody? Here ya go, bud."

I sighed indignantly inside the mask. Panic started to give way to frustration. I ripped the pen from his hand, signed the book, and shoved it back into the hands of the guest.

"Thanks, *bud*," said the boy, sarcastically imitating the attendant and giving me a punch on the arm.

My frustration had now turned to all-out anger. I pulled an invisible gun out of the empty holster that was strung on my costume belt. We weren't allowed to point our weapons—invisible or not—at guests, so I raised the barrel toward the giant cowboy reflection in the picture window and squeezed the trigger. As I did, I realized the pain in my upper body had subsided—or maybe I was just too mad to notice. I was breathing much easier, having been distracted from my uncomfortable situation by the annoyances around me. I shrugged my shoulders—as much as I could—and decided to simply "push through."

I made it to the end and never once buckled my head again in a Woody-set.

"Need your head snapped on," an attendant would inevitably ask as I headed onstage.

"Nope, got it," I'd say.

"How'd you reach by yourself?"

"I'm flexible."

"You want me to make sure it's fastened?"

I'd shake my head no—free and clear of any hindrance or pain. "If it comes loose, I'll give ya the SOS."

In addition to the Pixar shifts, I also took my cowboy act to Splash Mountain. In the Magic Kingdom, Buzz was replaced by Jessie, and the two of us had a big ol' time rounding up guests with our imaginary lassos and shooting our non-existent pistols into the sky in celebratory fashion anytime we spotted a birthday or anniversary pin. Our break room was off to the side of the attraction, behind the train tracks. The Keys to the Kingdom tours would often enter the backstage area through that particular cast entrance, and I always made a point—if I spotted a group going to or from set—to remove my Woody head, in order to give them a *real* behind-the-scenes moment. The guests thought it was the greatest, seeing the magic "unmasked"—a real-life Disney character without his head on. They'd all slip their phones out and try to sneak a couple pictures without their guide seeing. It was the only time we, as performers, were allowed to be seen by a guest without being "show ready" and not get fired for it—though if a manager saw you "showing off" by treating the guests to a Disney-peep-show, you'd get scolded anyhow.

I always remembered taking one of the tours myself as a young guest and seeing a headless character and being absolutely tickled by the experience, telling all my friends and family afterward and fancying myself a true Disney insider. I simply wanted to create a little of that backstage magic myself whenever I had the opportunity. Plus, anything to get that damn head off.

Despite breaking Wardrobe rules, and refusing to lock my mask into place, the costume eventually wore me down, and I got to the point where I—and especially my shoulders—dreaded seeing ol' Pull-String on the weekly schedule.

I was complaining about it one day to Jessie, and she offered a simple solution. "Just get disapproved," she told me.

"What do you mean?"

"Tell them the costume causes you pain, and they'll disapprove you."

"And take away all my Woody shifts?"

"Yep."

"Just like that?"

"I did it with King Louie. Allergic to the fur—or, at least, I told them I was."

On the day of my next Woody shift, I showed up to the Studios' Character Base early and inquired about the disapproval process. They sent me to speak with a manager. I sat at her desk and explained the type of pain that the head had been causing my shoulders. She let me make my case, then told me to head over to Wardrobe and get into full-costume.

"I'll be over in ten to check it out," she said.

"Thank you so much."

"Well, I haven't done anything yet," she reminded. "Maybe there's a quick fix."

If by quick fix you mean shoulder surgery, I thought to myself as I made my way to Costuming.

I pulled the costume from the rack and—thankfully, for the last time of my character-performer career—put on the cowboy suit.

The moment the manager arrived and saw how the head was knifing into my shoulder blades, she cringed and OK'd the disapproval. She seemed somber about the whole thing, as if trying to protect my feelings, like I'd just been fired or something.

I'd never been so happy in my life to be rejected.

I mean, it was slightly bittersweet hanging up the spurs for the last time. *Toy Story* was one of my favorite films, and Woody was such an iconic character. (Speaking of, did you know that Tom Hanks signed the wall over at...oh, wait, you did...okay, sorry.) But, in the end, I just couldn't shoulder the burden—literally—that came with playing everyone's favorite toy cowboy. I was relieved to have my schedule wiped clean of all such shifts, and more than a little thrilled when that day's shift was converted on-the-spot to a "spare" shift.

I made my way back to Character Base and enjoyed a cup of coffee until the scheduler sent me back to wardrobe to GAM-up. Heading outside a few minutes later to catch my golf cart, I turned back at the building's exit and, in full soldier-garb, gave a last salute to the lifeless Woody costume waiting to be returned to the rack. As I marched off, I could almost hear the twenty-one-gun salute of invisible six-shooters sounding their final tribute to my short-lived cowboy career.

CHAPTER SEVEN

The Two Bears

I didn't often get the chance to play *bear*, but over the years was able to get my Baloo on every now and then at the Animal Kingdom, and very rarely my Br'er Bear over at MK.

Baloo was a no-nonsense costume that I'd been familiar with since training. The shifts were generally in Africa with a King Louie pairing, but every so often I'd be scheduled for main-entrance shifts—DAK's version of a Hat set, in which a set of random characters lined up to greet guests entering the park. Technically, we were *outside* of the park, setting up camp on the cement area between bag check and the turnstiles.

The sets were relatively low-key, as many guests were too anxious to get into the park to stop and do a meet-and-greet. Still, enough eager kids were able to divert their parents away from the entrance and into the character lines that I got very good—and very fast—at my Baloo signature.

The only time anything out of the ordinary happened was when I was chased off set by a punk kid, probably thirteen years of age. He was the last guest in my line and greeted me with a hearty shove. The character attendant, who had his hands full watching over several characters, happened to see the incident and gave the boy a nice, calm Disney reprimand. Once the attendant had turned his back, however, the kid gave me a swift kick in the shin. Of course, his parents were nowhere to be found, so I simply took matters into my own hands.

I handed back his autograph book unsigned, turned, and walked quickly to the backstage entrance.

He followed, trying to trip me the whole way.

Thankfully, I was much bigger than him—especially with the costume—and was able to keep my balance.

He finally resorted to pulling my little nub of a tail as I went.

I was afraid if he tugged too hard, he may just pull the thing off, so I kept wiggling my butt while I walked to prevent him from getting a good hold on it. I passed a couple of sisters holding hands, and they thought I was trying to start up a dance party, so they quickly joined in. I moved around the pair, using them as a human shield to block my pursuer, then bolted for backstage.

The boy followed, but there was another cast of characters and an attendant waiting in the wings, who greeted the troublemaker with a boisterous, *non-Disney* reprimand, considering how we were out of the view of guests. The scolding seemed to scare him badly, and by the time the attendant had raised her walkie-talkie to her mouth, threatening to call security on him, the kid was long gone.

Some character performers liked to exact their own revenge on unruly or disrespectful guests. The King Louie who had bid the Africa location was a short, but very muscular, man with a fiery temper. The orangutan suit was designed with extra-long arms that extended far beyond the performer's, and were "controlled" by stick-like handles that began about midway through the costume arms. Anytime a guest was misbehaving, King Louie would make use of his long limbs by swinging around one of his hard, plastic hands and knocking a guest on the back of the head—or, sometimes swatting him or her on the behind. I always expected him to get in trouble for it—either by management or being sued by a guest—but it never happened. His character was technically a villain, and guests usually just laughed off the cheap shots as part of the act.

Every so often, a child would take offense and start crying. King Louie would simply wrap the kid up in his long arms with a great big ape hug and play the whole thing off as an accident. He'd act very remorseful and be extremely kind and gentle with the child, making them forget all about his tendency toward violence. Then, a couple guests later, he'd start swatting away again. He also liked to maintain the role's authenticity when it came to the climbing tendencies of his orangutan-alter-ego, turning the wooden structure under which we greeted guests into something of a jungle gym.

I never minded him taking all the attention on set; it meant far less work for me. I just stood there enjoying the swatting-crying-climbing show, signing the occasional autograph, and scratching my back against one of the structure's supporting wooden poles from time-to-time. Apparently, King Louie got the wrong idea and mistook my amused watching and waiting to see if he broke his neck—or any of the guest's—for flirtatious staring, and started asking me out on a regular basis.

Flik, from *A Bug's Life*, who shared a dressing room with us and spent every minute of her set breaks with her Bible open on her lap, reading, studying, and highlighting away, would flash him the dirtiest looks anytime he did so.

This ended up being a terrible idea—for both her and me—as King Louie started to tease her relentlessly about being *jealous*, and that *she* was the one who wanted to get with Baloo. Thus, she began including me in her death-stares to prove that this was *not* the case, and anytime I took a seat anywhere in her vicinity, she and her Bible would up and move to the other side of the room for good measure.

Every now and then at the Animal Kingdom, I'd get pulled from a shift to help out a short-handed parade crew. Generally, I'd be placed backstage at the parade's starting location and tasked with "rope and water" duties. This meant that I filled twenty or thirty plastic water cups and distributed them to the line of performers waiting to go on—after which, I'd carry one end of the rope that trailed the last float and signaled to guests the end of the parade.

One such afternoon, I was making my way down the line of performers, passing out water, when I saw my least favorite ant—Bible and Flik-suit free—high atop a pair of stilts. I purposely avoided her, until she asked directly for a cup. When she saw that it was me, she let loose one of her hellfire-and-damnation looks. Of course, I took my sweet time obliging her request, continuing to service the rest of the line ahead of her. Finally, a matter of seconds before the parade took off, I begrudgingly walked over and handed up a half-empty cup of water.

Less frequent still were my stints as *that other bear*—the one most guests referred to as Splash Mountain or The Bad Guy in That Racist Movie. Br'er Bear didn't make a whole lot of appearances in the park in general, so my experience with him was limited to only a handful of times in what was by far the heaviest of any costume that I wore.

Most of the larger—or fatter—character costumes had an inner plastic skeleton of sorts, made up of what were referred to as "costume rings." The rings provided support for the heavy fabric and kept the general rounded shape of the oversized character intact. The prep time for Br'er Bear—thanks to the countless number of rings that had to be inserted and fastened from top to bottom of the long, tall torso—was extensive.

On the outside, there wasn't much to the costume at all, besides the fur, a sewn-on hat, and a size-XXXXXL

blue shirt that was worn unbuttoned. It was a good thing
the original character had not been drawn with a full-
blown outfit or any accessories; the thick fur coat alone
was enough to weigh down even the most muscly of character performers—which wasn't me. The first time I wore
the costume, I had to be careful to conserve my steps; it
took a great deal of effort just to pick up one furry bear
paw and put it in front of the other, especially compared
to the hip-hugging spandex that doubled as my usual
dog skin. *If it wasn't neck problems, it was knee problems.*

That wasn't the only trouble I had with the costume. My
very first set, I was out with Br'er Rabbit. Getting into
our roles, my partner would tease me, hide from me,
maybe tap me on the shoulder, then disappear before
I—the bumbling bear villain—turned around. I'd play
dumb, scratch my head in bewilderment, before he (who
was really a *she*) would spring out and scare me, and we'd
have a good laugh together. The guests seemed to love
the sort of Laurel-and-Hardy slapstick thing we had going. But, each time we made our way through another
bit, raising our paws to our mouths and beginning the
classic, over-exaggerated "character laugh," Br'er Rabbit
would grow awkward. She'd stop midway through, shake
her head, and walk away. I didn't understand what she
was doing or how it fit into our playful routine. I started
getting fed up with her as a partner, wondering why she
insisted on cutting short the comedy. I kept at it.

I started play-chasing her around a trash can—arms
outstretched, taking heavy, plodding, oaf-like steps as
I ran slow circles in pursuit.

She took the bait and joined in. After a couple laps, she
ducked down behind the trash can, then sprang up to
surprise me.

I fake-stumbled around like I'd lost my bearings (no
pun intended), while my partner erupted in laughter,

howling and pointing at the big, dumb bear she'd managed to outwit yet again. I kicked at the ground, acting as if I was mad that I'd failed to catch my adversary, then went into a hearty belly laugh myself. I put both paws up to the bear's mouth and started to bob and shake inside the massive costume to get the desired effect.

Br'er Rabbit stopped yet again, raised her hands questioningly, then walked over and began consoling a nearby toddler. The young guest had at first been amused by our charade, but her laughter had fallen silent, and she now seemed on the verge of tears.

I hung my head and returned to greeting guests.

Anytime I came near after that, Br'er Rabbit "playfully" pushed me away, refusing to engage in any more shenanigans.

When the set was over, we headed backstage, and before we even began removing our costumes, I asked her why she'd given me the cold shoulder.

"You were being weird," she replied, sounding like she was still annoyed.

"What do you mean?"

"Kinda morbid for Disney, don't you think?"

I had no idea what she was talking about and so repeated my question.

"Acting like you wanna kill me in front of all those kids," she said.

"Huh?"

"Like you're gonna strangle me." She wrapped her hands around her furry rabbit neck and shook them like she was choking herself.

A light bulb suddenly switched on. "Ohhh," I said, "I was *laughing*!"

"*Laughing?*"

"How did you not get that?"

"Because you weren't laughing, you were strangling."

I raised my hands to demonstrate and began shaking

and gyrating to imitate a bear-sized fit of laughter.

She swatted me in the gut. "Stop!"

"What's wrong with my laugh?" I demanded to know. "Hands over mouth, bob and shake, just like we were taught."

"Your mouth's up there," she said in a biting tone, pointing her finger about a foot above my head.

I paused and thought for a moment, then ripped off my mask to inspect.

My face turned red. *Damn*. She was right.

Up to that point, the tallest costume I'd been in was Goofy, whose open mouth doubled as the performer's view screen. Nearly all of my character heads were built the same way, save Br'er Bear and his fur-colored *neck* screen. I reached high above my head and felt the elusive jawline. *Oops*.

Br'er Rabbit was correct: I had been *very* weird onstage, clutching at my throat and convulsing over and over again during the set...to the *non*-delight of her and all the guests watching. Some character laugh.

Guess the joke was on me.

CHAPTER EIGHT

The Monster

Another costume to rival the size and weight of Br'er Bear was Sully from *Monsters, Inc.* I was thrilled to pick up another Pixar character, seeing as how things hadn't worked out between me and Woody. The nature of the Sully outfit made it the only one that required extensive help from the character attendant. We're not talking about a quick tuck of neck fur, but the all-out lifting and placing of the upper body onto the lower half...kind of like a real-life Matryoshka doll. (Open the big monster and there's a small human inside!) Sully's proportions also required the use of "arm-poles" a la King Louie, in order to control the character's extra-long limbs. This, of course, meant no autograph to learn or sign. Fine by me. It also meant that a twelve-year-old boy who came to visit ended up with a pair of broken glasses.

I used the arm-poles to wrap kids up in monster hugs, or if I was very careful, to pat little ones on the head. But when I whipped an arm up and back to try and rest it on the shoulders of a young guest as we posed side-by-side for a photo, I misjudged his height and didn't quite clear his head. The molded blue plastic that made up the hand at the end of the long, furry arm smacked hard against the kid's glasses, and a crack rang out through the set location. I immediately dropped my arm, praying the cringe-worthy sound hadn't been that of a fractured skull. Thankfully, the little guy was a trooper. He stood squinting and blinking away the pain, with a bit of a grin still left on his face.

"Don't worry. It's not the first time that's happened," his mother said, stepping forward and removing the glasses from her son's face.

"It's the first time they've been broken by a monster, I bet," said the character attendant, trying to lighten the mood.

The boy laughed. "Uh-huh," he said, suddenly proud to have been clocked by a cartoon movie star.

My set partner, Mike Wazowski, approached, pointing at his giant eyeball.

The character attendant translated. "Mike says he's only got *one* eye, so glasses or not, you're still doing better than him."

The mom chuckled at the joke and patted her smiling son on the head.

We all posed for a few pictures, and the family left, thankfully having forgotten all about my unintentional assault on their son.

I patted my little green friend on the back to thank him (her) for helping to smooth over the mishap.

My partner unfortunately knew all about onstage humiliation, as I discovered later that day while the two of us chatted in the break room.

I came to find out that she was *the* Mike Wazowski of cast member lore and internet fame who had been captured by a guest's video camera as she tripped over her monster-feet and face-planted on the concrete floor. Her giant eyeball shattered upon impact and her round shell-of-a-costume rendered her immobile—like a turtle flipped belly-up on its shell—and so she had no choice but to lay there in a pool of shame and broken plastic until the PhotoPass photographer came to her aid.

She was hesitant in revealing her identity as the Falling Mike, since the video had gone viral and her hilarious misstep was now brought up as a teaching point during every character's training week. But I think she felt bad for me, since I'd just punched out a pre-teen, and so divulged—in hushed tones—her true identity.

I suddenly didn't feel as bad about my blunder. As soon as Wazowski went back to reading her book, I retrieved my phone and pretended to text, but instead pulled the video up on YouTube and watched it several times. That really cleared my conscience, as I struggled to hold in the laughter.

On my fourth viewing, a thought struck me. "Did you have to pay for the costume?" I asked.

She looked up from her book and shook her head no.

"My trainer told me the Mike costume costs fif-ty-thou..."

She interrupted me by laughing and shaking her head more emphatically. "Someone else told me that. Pretty sure Entertainment started saying that after I fell. You know, to scare performers and get them to be more careful."

"Bastards."

She smiled and went back to her book.

I watched the video one more time, then texted my training buddy the truth about the high-priced costume rumor. Of course, I also had to brag that I was sitting in the same room as Falling Mike.

The Monsters off-set location was another closet-sized dressing room, tucked away at the back of the Studios in the Streets of America. It was dark and dingy, and considering the unusual shape and size of both Mike and Sully's costumes, had almost no room for the performers to relax. I usually took the lone folding metal chair, while Mike stretched out on a large shelf, as if it were a bunk bed.

The sets were never overly busy, the location being somewhat out of the way from most guest traffic. I eventually got used to the arm-poles and decided they made for a fun break from the norm of jointed elbows and opposable thumbs. Of course, I was responsible for a few more cheap shots here and there, but nothing that an apologetic, furry hug couldn't resolve. The company was usually good. I mean, meeting Falling Mike was a treat in itself, but most of the other Wazowskis were easy to get along with as well.

There was one that I could have done without. She was on her phone constantly, and even smuggled it onstage so she could continue using it inside her "green bubble" throughout the set. She told me that she and some of her coworkers—both male and female—had a sort of running game of phone tag, in which they'd text one another pictures of their "bits and pieces" while changing in and out of their costumes. It was slightly disturbing, while on-set hugging a happy family, to look down and see a lifeless Mike, and know my partner was inside swiping through penis pics.

She asked once after a set if I wanted to join in the fun. I told her I was worried that ongoing sexting may put a damper on the magic for me personally and politely declined the offer.

For a laugh, I did volunteer my training buddy's phone number, telling Horny Mike that a certain space ranger I knew would most certainly be game.

CHAPTER NINE

The Beast

I ended up making my way 'round to World Showcase now and again after my training days, thanks to my friend, the Beast. It was my only experience working alongside a face character (non-costumed character performers, such as the princes and princesses), which took most of the pressure off me, since Belle maintained an ongoing conversation with the guests throughout the interaction and even signed autographs for the both of us.

The costume was another of the extra-large variety, and the amount of fur and clothing mixed with the lack of shade at the outdoor set location in Epcot's France pavilion made for hellish temperatures inside the outfit. In fact, those who had *Beast-ed* before me came up with an ingenious system for making it through the sweaty sets, and luckily I was informed by my switch-out upon arrival how to survive the coming shift.

"Put your paws in the freezer," said Beast #1, nodding in the direction of the combination refrigerator-freezer on one end of the break room.

"Yeah?"

"And your skull cap and t-shirt if you want."

"I'm in. Too bad the head doesn't fit."

He smiled. "And, drink lots of…"

"No worries there," I said, trading out my costume pieces for a couple of Power-Ades.

"They'll be nice and icy by set-time," he promised, pulling on his own frosty paws and heading into the furnace.

"Thanks," I called after him, between chugs.

When the time arrived, I found the items to be shiver-worthy as I slipped into my half-frozen t-shirt. The paws came out a perfect thirty-two degrees, with little ice crystals starting to form amidst the clumps of fur. The trick kept my hands, head, and chest cool for nearly half the set, ensuring the prevention of a heat stroke in the Florida sun. I never played the Beast again without chilling before serving.

Speaking of heat, during one France shift, Belle and I ran up against a midlife-crisis father who had a serious thing for the Beauty-half of our duo. He was standing toward the back of the line with his two sons; they looked to be about fourteen or fifteen. "You're hot!" the man screamed at my partner, before dying laughing with his boys, who apparently shared with their dad his sense of humor, as well as his intellectual capacity.

"Is he talking to *you*?" said the six-year-old girl who was currently wrapped up in a hug from her favorite princess.

Belle winked and said, "I didn't hear a thing."

The little girl giggled and asked for an autograph.

"You're hot, Belle!"

"I think he's talking to *you*," the little girl insisted.

Belle stayed in character. "I used to have to put up with the same thing from Gaston," she said, rolling her eyes and sighing.

"Gaston's mean!" cried the little girl.

"He sure is, Princess," replied Belle with a smile.

"Belle! Belle! Belle! Belle!" the man started to chant.

"*You're* mean!" shouted the little girl, as she turned and pointed a chubby little finger in his direction.

Those guests in line who'd already been giving him dirty looks now turned as one and told him to get lost.

The attention made him rowdier. "Come on, Belle, I'll show you *my* beast," he and his doomed progeny erupted.

The parents with small children were now downright angry and became more vocal about the troublemaker leaving. "This is *Disney World*, not a strip club!" someone said. "Go back to the Biergarten," suggested another.

Our character attendant—a sixty-something man, who was sweet and soft-spoken, probably a retired snowbird that picked up winter shifts at the parks—sighed deeply and headed back to say a few words to the man.

"Sorry for that," he said to us in a solemn voice when he returned. "He shouldn't be a prob—"

"Lose your bodyguards," came another shout from the back, as the guest motioned toward me and the attendant, "and come home to my castle."

The attendant grabbed his walkie-talkie so fast, I thought he might be planning on chucking it at the jerk's head like a ninja star. He didn't...unfortunately. Instead, he spat some code into the mouthpiece, and literally twenty-seconds later, two plain-clothes security officers descended upon the scene.

The whole line watched with a mix of shock and relief as they ushered him and his sons away.

"Follow us; we'll escort you out of the park," said one of the men, as they went.

"I paid good money for these tickets," the man protested.

"So did we!" someone from the line shouted, which brought about more than a few laughs.

The crowd broke into applause.

The character attendant couldn't stop blushing as Belle and many of the guests thanked him for handling the situation. Had I been able to talk, I would have done the same.

The little girl, whose meet-and-greet had been interrupted, said enough for all of us, however, as she made a point to hug all three of her heroes—Beauty, the Beast, *and* the character attendant—before skipping off down the streets of Paris.

CHAPTER TEN

The Pirate

In addition to my stints in magical kingdoms and foreign lands, my duties every so often took me away from land altogether. As in water. As in *pirates*. And we're no longer talking about plastic swords and dog-ear earrings, but the real deal: the one-handed, mustachioed variety who do their best to keep a straight face around sharp-toothed reptilians. That's right, the captain himself (the *original* captain...sorry, Jack). *Hook*.

I only played the villain a couple of times, both shifts at the Contemporary Resort for the Pirates and Pals Fireworks Voyage. On the first occasion, I had no idea what to expect during the extra-long van ride over from Character Base to the hotel. The costume had been pre-packed for me, so I hadn't even had the chance to familiarize myself with it before being shown up a back staircase, through a series of empty ballrooms, and into the tiny space designated as the character dressing room. It looked as if cast members of the hotel—maybe housekeeping or kitchen staff—also made use of the space, based on the various personal effects and costume pieces left lying around.

My partner, Mr. Smee, was being played by a college-age girl who'd done the gig countless times before and was thus far more interested in the screen of her phone than anything that was happening around her in real life. I did manage to coax a few words out of her, in regard to the placement of the lacy kerchief that adorned Hook's neck, as well as a rough idea of the captain's signature.

For some reason, I'd never been tested on it in training and hadn't thought to study up before the shift, figuring they'd have examples waiting for me, as they always did when a performer was scheduled in a role for the first time. Being a non-park shift, however, and with the binders full of those types of resources stowed at the various Character Bases, I had no such luck. Smee sketched her best estimation of the Hook signature on the back of her Calculus homework and handed over the sheet of notebook paper for me to practice.

"Wait..." I said, panicking slightly, "Which hand gets the *hook*."

"Left," she said.

I breathed a sigh of relief. "Thank god. No way I could do this cursive with my left."

I didn't have long, but I was able to master the relatively straightforward signature by the time our attendant gave the five-minute warning.

I finished dressing, slipping on my face, and then hook and glove. Looking myself over in the mirror, I realized I'd never played an out-and-out villain before. I mean, technically Br'er Bear was a villain, but he was little more than a hapless, oversized teddy bear. Hook was my first *real* bad guy, and it suddenly occurred to me that the overly affectionate, lovable, over-the-top personalities I sported for my regular cast of characters wouldn't cut it for Hook.

"What should I do?" I asked the attendant nervously, as we descended the stairs to the onstage location.

"What do you mean?"

"I've never been Hook before," I admitted.

"Really?" he said, sounding shocked. "Just make trouble."

"Ooo... kay." *Thanks for your help*, I thought.

"Just follow my lead," chimed in Smee.

"Got it," I said, as I grabbed the staircase railing with my left hand to steady myself and those big ol' pirate boots. I forgot I didn't have a left hand and almost took a tumble, but thankfully caught myself by slamming into the attendant on the step below me.

He turned around to make sure I was alright, but not without sighing loudly and rolling his eyes.

He led us out of the stairwell and through a big open room that was used for conventions and special events, then paused at the next set of doors. "Set location's on the other side. Forty minutes or so of meet-and-greets," he said unenthusiastically.

"Only one set?" I asked unbelievingly.

"Yep," he said, flinging open the doors to an upper-floor, lobby-type area full of milling guests.

I couldn't believe my luck: a single set. I could definitely get used to shifts like this. Plus, no sun and a swanky hotel...a pirate's life for me.

I followed Smee out and took my place alongside her against a wall. The guests—mostly families with young children who were dressed as pirates themselves—quickly formed a long line.

Smee immediately swiped the first autograph book offered in our direction and hid it behind her back. The kids started giggling and raced around her to retrieve it. She then held it high overhead, until they started jumping up and down like trained seals.

I took my cue from her mischievous villain act and began pacing circles around the children, stroking my chin and mustache as if I was sizing them up for a good old-fashioned sword fight.

Once Smee finally relented and signed the book, the oldest child timidly extended the souvenir forward in my direction.

I waved the book off, as if I wasn't the least bit interested, and started paying attention to the other children.

The boy persistently tugged on my sleeve.

I snobbishly brushed at my sleeve as if he'd just soiled my captain's jacket with his grubby little hands. Being a villain was fun!

After another thirty seconds of ignoring him, I finally ripped the book from his hands, acting as bothered as possible while attempting to flip to a blank page. Except I had no hands left to do so. I fumbled about and the collision of book, hand, and hook ended with Mr. Smee retrieving the book from the floor, turning to an open page, and placing and holding it on my left forearm for me while I signed. *Thank god.*

I received the assistance of my first mate for the next five or six families, until I was well enough acquainted with the drill that I was able to slowly and carefully do it myself. *So much for my tough-guy villain act.* The whole devil-may-care attitude just wasn't coming off as well, having to bend over and pick up dropped autograph books every ten seconds.

I gave it my best shot, and eventually made it through the line.

After the final family had taken their photos and received their illegible autographs, I saw the attendant approaching and felt relieved to be finished.

"Time to head out," he said.

I nodded and readied to return backstage.

He saw me take a step in that direction and stopped me. "*Outside,*" he clarified.

Outside? What the hell did that mean? Were we riding back to Character Base *in costume*?

"Take this," he said, handing over a two-foot-long stick flying a pirate flag.

I raised my hands to question.

"We're going to the boat," he whispered, like it was the most obvious thing in the world.

Boat?!

"I forgot you've never done this," he continued in a hushed voice. "I'll lead you from up ahead; just keep an eye out."

He took off at a quick pace to get a head start. Meanwhile, the crowd had started to excitedly gather around.

Not knowing what to do, I hoisted the flag high overhead, and the guests broke into cheering. I began to march, Smee in tow, the many guests falling in line behind. I kept a keen eye on the attendant about twenty yards ahead.

The nature of the gig was so bizarre and foreign to me. Sure, I'd experienced a long leash on GAM shifts, but this was character freedom on another level. I watched dumbfounded as the attendant hopped on an escalator and disappeared from sight. Smee and I followed suit with scores of giddy children and their parents close on our heels. I turned around to look at the packed moving stairs and gave a little wave of the flag. A cheer went up.

The attendant led us for what seemed like the length of the entire building before exiting some glass doors onto the hotel grounds. The sun had set, and it was a bit of a challenge navigating the landscaping and walkways in long coat, boots, and a mask that intensified the darkness tenfold.

The glow from the moon and the small outdoor lights that illuminated the sidewalks were just enough to keep the attendant barely visible. He headed straight for the Seven Seas Lagoon before finally disappearing into the mist.

I continued in that direction until I came to the edge of a long pier. Not knowing what to do, I paused. I felt Smee pushing me onward, and so I stepped out onto the pier, as wobbly and unsure as if I was being made to walk the plank. Thankfully, a few steps down the dock, the attendant once more came into view. He was twenty paces dead ahead, standing next to a sizable watercraft.

Still oblivious to the specifics of my role in all of this, I pressed onward. Nearing, I saw that a small gangplank had been lowered to provide access to the boat. I stepped onto the gangplank and began boarding.

I suddenly felt a hard tug on my sleeve. It was the attendant pulling me back from the boat. "Not you!" he shout-whispered.

I retreated and was forcefully directed to a spot off to the side of the gangplank, where I stood stiffly, waving my flag at the parade of guests who boarded in my stead.

Once the last of them had passed, the gangplank was raised by a couple of Transportation cast members, and the lot of them sailed away for a special viewing of the Magic Kingdom's nightly Wishes presentation.

The three of us alone again, I raised my arms in question, waiting for the next set of orders.

The attendant snatched the flag from me. "Let's load up," he said, and hastily set off down the dock, back toward the hotel.

On one hand, I was disappointed that I didn't get to set sail with the rest of my crew, but on the other, I was sick of being in the *dark*—both literally and figuratively—and ready to be done with a costume and shift I knew nothing about.

On the van ride home, I thanked Smee and the attendant for getting me through my first Hook shift. I reached in my black bag and retrieved the folded-up math homework that belonged to my partner. "You'll probably want this back," I said, passing it forward to the bench seat, where Smee lay stretched out, playing on her phone.

She grabbed it and stuffed it into her backpack with one hand. "What'd ya think?"

"Short and sweet," I said.

"The best kind of shift."

"I'll do better next time. Just took a little while to get my sea legs," I joked.

Both Smee and the attendant remained silent, as if maybe they were hoping there wouldn't be a next time.

Thankfully, there was only one more next time, with a different partner and attendant.

In true character-performer fashion (trying to survive in the Mouse-eat-Mouse world of Disney Entertainment was a full-time job in and of itself at times), I acted like an old pro. By my overdone confidence and the amount of time I spent playing on my phone acting disinterested in the goings-on around me, you'd think that I'd played pirate at the Contemp my whole life.

My Smee was a greenhorn and visibly nervous waiting to go on set. I, on the other hand, was completely unbothered. With an arrogant twist of my mustache, I turned my plastic nose up and reached for the door that led onstage. "Follow my lead," I said, strutting out a seasoned villain.

CHAPTER ELEVEN

Last Meal

I never fell in love with those random, miscella-neous-type shifts, scattered throughout Disney proper-ty. Aside from Hook, I was made to endure them from time-to-time on the dining circuit—though I tried my very best not to. Character dining was the absolute worst. It was love-and-shove to the Nth degree. Not to mention, there were maps involved. As a character per-former, anytime you were provided a visual aid to ex-plain how and where a particular set was to take place, establishing the expectation for you to subsequently navigate, while visually and physically impaired, the particulars of said pre-established route...you knew you it was gonna be a long set.

The first time I was scheduled at a restaurant, I showed up at the Animal Kingdom's Tusker House, changed into my Goofy costume, and set about studying the din-ing-room map provided by my attendant. Perhaps, if the penciled-in route had followed a logical sequence around the restaurant, I'd have been fine. The zig-zags randomly connecting the tables on the sheet before me, however, looked like the erratic lines of a polygraph printout if a Disney manager had asked me whether or not I enjoyed dining shifts. Onstage, trying to remember the order of tables, amidst a full house of highchairs and free-roam-ing children blocking the route at every turn, made for an absolute nightmare. Plus, if I spent more than fifteen seconds at a table, the overseeing attendant would approach from the corner of the room and hustle me along.

After the first set, the impatient attendant received a radio call from his manager complaining about the time it took to get through that particular seating of guests. Before answering, he looked at me angrily. "I told you to speed it up," he said.

"You saw me—I was going as fast as I could."

He softened a bit. "I know," he admitted.

"These people paid hundreds of dollars for this. I can't just fist-bump them as I walk by their table."

He shook his head understandingly, but the look on his face seemed torn between the business-side and magic-side of his duties. He spoke into his walkie-talkie. "It's *really* busy in there. We'll do what we can to make up time."

"What we can to make up time" ended up being me working an extra half-hour over my scheduled shift time out of the goodness of my heart—and by "out of the goodness of my heart," I mean out of the fear of me and my attendant getting canned over a breakfast of Mickey-shaped waffles.

After that experience, I started trading all my Tusker-House shifts to fellow cast members. Believe it or not, there were those out there who enjoyed the fast-paced love-em-and-leave-em world of dining. I'd heard similar stories about Chef Mickey's, and since I'd already had my fill of confusion and uncertainty at the Contemporary, I never even gave it a shot, swapping every last one of the shifts that appeared on my schedule. I did give the Swan and Dolphin character dinner a shot...once.

Luckily, it was an extremely slow night—three or four tables total—so no pressure, prodding attendant, or map, thank god. Also, there was hardly anyone to witness me try to clear a low doorway in my seven-foot-plus Goofy costume and nearly behead myself. Yes, both of them: plastic *and* human. The blow was enough to give me a migraine and to remind me never to do another dining shift as long as I lived. So, I didn't.

It wasn't long after that the real world came calling, anyway—grad school, in particular—to coax me out of my costume and back into an adult wardrobe. While I'd loved practically living in the Most Magical Place on Earth and doing my small part to carry on Walt's legacy—helping to set the stage for the company's eventual world-take-over—I had dreams of my own that needed tending.

My last character shift was appropriately scheduled at Epcot—where it had all started back in training—in, what else, but the ol' Goof costume. It was uneventful, but memorable all the same: a standard, straightforward C-Spot shift, capped off with a wave of memories and nostalgia as I scanned in my costume and threw my dirty basics into the laundry bins one final time.

I smiled at the naked, sweaty face in the mirror on the wall and took a big whiff of that distinct Costuming smell with me, as I headed out to the backstage parking lot and drove away, half-empty bottle of blue Power-Ade resting in my cup holder.

Epilogue

Visiting Walt Disney World nowadays—and I do so more frequently than ever—is like coming home, revisiting the old town where I used to live. And, only the best parts...none of the headaches, or neck pains, or cranky managers. My heart always flutters in pride and recognition at the sight of a character performer—whether it be the pirate, beast, monster, either of the two bears, cowboy, soldier, superhero, or of course that wonderfully clumsy, big-headed dog.

And, yes, I still pop my foot out to the side, toe pointed skyward, when posing for pictures at the parks, as if my old trainer was hiding, waiting to spring out and critique my form. As if I was still one of them. One of...*us*.

I guess you can take the man out of the Mouse, but never the Mouse out of the man.

About the Author

Nicklaus Hopkins makes his living as a professional writer and college professor. His work has appeared in over forty television shows and numerous print publications. He and his wife, who is also an author, reside in central Florida and visit the Mouse as often as possible.

About Theme Park Press

Theme Park Press publishes books primarily about the Disney company, its history, culture, films, animation, and theme parks, as well as theme parks in general.

Our authors include noted historians, animators, Imagineers, and experts in the theme park industry.

We also publish many books by first-time authors, with topics ranging from fiction to theme park guides.

And we're always looking for new talent. If you'd like to write for us, or if you're interested in the many other titles in our catalog, please visit:

www.ThemeParkPress.com

. . . .

Theme Park Press Newsletter

Subscribe to our free email newsletter and enjoy:

- ◆ Free book downloads and giveaways
- ◆ Access to excerpts from our many books
- ◆ Announcements of forthcoming releases
- ◆ Exclusive additional content and chapters
- ◆ And more good stuff available nowhere else

To subscribe, visit www.ThemeParkPress.com, or send email to newsletter@themeparkpress.com.

Read more about these books
and our many other titles at:

www.ThemeParkPress.com